David Hare was born in Sussex in 1947. Upon leaving university he formed the Portable Theatre Company, which toured Britain for three years. He wrote his first play, *Slag* in 1970, while Literary Manager at the Royal Court Theatre. Since then he has written fourteen plays of which nine have been presented at the National Theatre, and seven original screenplays for cinema and television. His first feature film, *Wetherby*, won the Golden Bear at Berlin in 1985.

THE ABSENCE
OF WAR

DAVID HARE

faber and faber
LONDON · BOSTON

First published in Great Britain in 1993 by
Faber and Faber Limited 3 Queen Square London WCIN 3AU

Photoset by Parker Typesetting Service, Leicester
Printed in England by Clays Ltd, St Ives plc

A CIP record for this book
is available from the British Library

ISBN 0 571 17071 4

4 6 8 10 9 7 5 3

For Nicole

CHARACTERS

In the Leader's Office
RT HON GEORGE JONES MP
ANDREW BUCHAN, his minder
OLIVER DIX, his political adviser
GWENDA AARON, his diary secretary
MARY HOUSEGO, his press secretary
LINDSAY FONTAINE, his publicity adviser

Also in the Labour Party
RT HON MALCOLM PRYCE MP
BRUCE, his minder
RT HON BRYDEN THOMAS MP
VERA KLEIN

In the World Outside
LINUS FRANK
TREVOR AVERY
RT HON CHARLES KENDRICK MP

Parliament, the media, the military, etc.

The Absence of War was first performed at the Olivier Theatre on 2 October 1993 as the third part of the David Hare trilogy. The first two parts, *Racing Demon* and *Murmuring Judges* were performed on the same day. The cast was as follows:

The Leader's Office

THE RT HON. GEORGE JONES MP	John Thaw
ANDREW BUCHAN	Paul Moriarty
OLIVER DIX	Oliver Ford Davies
GWENDA AARON	Barbara Leigh-Hunt
MARY HOUSEGO	Saskia Wickham
LINDSAY FONTAINE	Clare Higgins

The Labour Party

THE RT HON. MALCOLM PRYCE MP	Richard Pasco
BRUCE	Adrian Scarborough
THE RT HON. BRYDEN THOMAS MP	Michael Bryant
VERA KLEIN	Maria Charles

The World Outside

LINUS FRANK	Robin Bailey
TREVOR AVERY	Tyrone Huggins
THE RT HON. CHARLES KENDRICK MP	Nicholas Day
CONSTABLE IN COMMONS	Edward Clayton
CAROLE KENDRICK	Judith Coke
MAKE-UP GIRL	Tacye Nichols
WAITRESS	Judy Damas

And	Doyne Byrd
	Peter Dineen
	Femi Elofowoju Jnr
	Chris Gascoyne
	Paul Gilmore
	Julie Hewlett
	Chook Sibtain
	Roger Swaine
	Robert Tunstall
Director	Richard Eyre
Designer	Bob Crowley
Lighting	Mark Henderson
Music	Richard Hartley

When people start making visionary speeches about the green hills far away, it is time to reach for your bicycle and cycle away.

JOHN MAJOR

It is observed that when a man is firm inside and gentle without, he is a healer. When he is hard outside and soft inside, he is useless.

AMERICAN INDIAN LEGEND

ACT ONE: HATS OFF, STRANGERS!

SCENE ONE

The Cenotaph. As the audience come in to the theatre, they see the Cenotaph Memorial dimly lit on stage with large flags at its base. As we arrive, so too do those who will take part in the ceremony – the soldiers, sailors, airmen and diplomats who stand on three sides to create an open area around the Memorial. The massed bands begin to play. Then, as the lights go down, the discreet voice of the distinguished broadcaster, LINUS FRANK, *is heard, as everyone on stage stands silent, waiting.*

LINUS FRANK: Welcome again to the annual ceremony of the Cenotaph where we remember the men and women of the Home Forces and of the Commonwealth who sacrificed themselves in the wars of this century in order that we may be allowed to live.
(There is a moment's silence. Then on to the stage in a procession of three walk the country's political leaders. First, the Prime Minister, CHARLES KENDRICK, *who is tall, grey-haired, in his early fifties. Behind him,* GEORGE JONES, *the Leader of the Opposition. He is the same age, apparently unassuming but thick-set and powerfully built. Behind them, the* LIBERAL LEADER, *shorter and younger. Each of the three wears an almost identical dark, heavy coat and each carries a wreath of poppies. With their backs to us, they are indistinguishable. They stand a moment, a line of three, isolated, before* LINUS FRANK *resumes.)*
If today all those who have died since 1914 fighting for this country were to parade four abreast past the Cenotaph, then the procession's head, now, at one minute to eleven, would be here in Whitehall, and its tail would stand waiting in Edinburgh.
(Now the music of massed bands swells over Whitehall, and the crowd is stilled as the wind stirs among them.)
Here on this, the eleventh day of the eleventh month at the eleventh hour, in country churches and by stone memorials on village greens, the people of this country are asked to join

with its leaders in two minutes' silence as we remember the price of freedom.

(*At this, Big Ben chimes. A gun fires in salute. The silence begins. After a few moments, a light finds* ANDREW BUCHAN, *at the side of the ceremony. He is heavily built, with spectacles and a thick coat. His bulk and pallor mean he could pass for anything between 25 and 45 years of age. He addresses us.*)

ANDREW: I love this moment. The two minutes' silence. It always moves me, year after year. It gives you a breath, just to question. The questions everyone in politics asks.

Why these hours? Why these ridiculous schedules? Up and out of our beds at six every day. Read the papers. When you know already what the papers will say. Grab a quick croissant – a croissant! Jesus, I'm from Paisley – then the first meeting of the day. Seven o'clock and I'm there.

And outside that meeting, another meeting, already beating, bulging, pressing against the door. Your mind's already on the next one, the one you are already late for, the one which may – God help us – achieve a little bit more than the one you are at now.

What is this for? This madness? To bed at twelve-thirty. After which the phone goes only twice. And once more at three-fifteen. As it happens, a wrong number. But you do not dare turn the thing off.

(*The guns fire again.* KENDRICK *steps forward and lays his wreath at the bottom of the memorial.* GEORGE *steps forward and lays his beside it. The* LIBERAL LEADER *steps forward and lays his alongside theirs. Then the three men stand a moment, heads bowed.* ANDREW *looks up.*)

I have a theory. People of my age, we did not fight in a war. If you fight in a war, you have some sense of personal worth. So now we seek it by keeping busy. We work and hope we will feel we do good.

(*At once, on this last word, the whole scene dissolves, the military and the politicians scatter and* ANDREW *leads us quickly to the Lobby of the House of Commons.*)

The lobby of the House of Commons. Four corridors meet in an octagonal Gothic space with marble statuary, and a tiled floor of many colours. To one side there is a desk, rather like a maître d's, and attended by men in tails and white ties and by a couple of POLICEMEN. *All around,* MPs, *summoned by the small chits they hold in their hands, are mingling and meeting with members of the public.* ANDREW BUCHAN *crosses quickly to meet* LINDSAY FONTAINE. LINDSAY *is in her mid-thirties, tall, articulate and quick-thinking.*

ANDREW: Lindsay, I'm sorry. I'm Andrew Buchan.

LINDSAY: Hello. Yes, I think we have met.

ANDREW: That's right. Briefly. At the health service benefit. Didn't you organize it?

LINDSAY: Sort of. Well, I did the campaign.

(ANDREW *stands a moment, apologetic.*)

ANDREW: George asked me to meet you. He's got Prime Minister's Questions. So he couldn't come. Then he was going to. Now he can't, I'm afraid. Though he still may if . . . (*He looks at his watch.*) Well now it's unlikely. (*He smiles at her.*) I act as his sweeper. Sheer weight of traffic, as the radio says.

(*They both smile, at ease.*)

LINDSAY: It's pretty hectic?

ANDREW: It's a problem with opposition. The government has cars. And teams of civil servants. Resources. Buildings. Access to the facts. But George has much less. He has only his own private office. (*He smiles.*) George has to make do with us.

(LINDSAY *smiles politely.*)

LINDSAY: Yes.

ANDREW: You've met George already?

LINDSAY: Only socially.

ANDREW: That's what I heard. He knew of course of the work you've been doing . . .

LINDSAY: This was a dinner party actually. It was just chance. I

3

had no idea that George would be there. It was given by some actors . . .

ANDREW: George loves the theatre.

LINDSAY: Yes. Well, he certainly does. (*She nods.*) I'd never met him. When you meet him of course he's fantastically impressive. I found myself wondering why am I surprised? He's so authoritative. Why should that surprise me?
(ANDREW *is smiling now.*)
I'm sure you've heard this kind of thing before.

ANDREW: Once or twice.

LINDSAY: Yes I'm sure it must be familiar. I didn't mean to start right in like this. But you meet George, you think: 'this man is dynamite'. So then you ask the next question. Why on earth does this never quite come across?
(ANDREW *looks at her a moment, as if deciding just how hard he is going to have to go in. But just as he starts decisively, he is interrupted.*)

ANDREW: Yeah. Look . . .
(*And at once* GWENDA AARON *appears. She is in her early fifties, in a pleated skirt and moving from one corridor to another. She is barely ever still.*)

GWENDA: You haven't seen George?

ANDREW: Isn't he with you?

GWENDA: No.

ANDREW: Oh God, has he gone walkabout? (*He turns despairingly to introduce them.*) This is George's secretary, Gwenda. This is Lindsay Fontaine.

LINDSAY: How do you do?
(*But* GWENDA *just smiles vaguely at her.*)

ANDREW: He did his lunch, did he? The city lunch. (*To* LINDSAY.) George was massaging banks. For the big moment.

GWENDA: That's where we lost him. He went to get tobacco.

ANDREW: The driver let him go? How could he? Doesn't he know? (*He turns away, making himself angry by repetition.*) Hasn't anyone *told* him?

GWENDA: He's been told. A thousand times. There's one rule with George. Never slacken the leash.

4

(Before ANDREW *can respond he finds two men in impeccable suits heading towards him.* MALCOLM PRYCE MP *is in his late forties, laconic, smooth and extremely sharp. His minder,* BRUCE, *is immediately behind him, pencil-thin, young.)*

MALCOLM: There you are, Andrew.

ANDREW: Malcolm.

GWENDA: I'm going.

(Saying this, she has already headed off, a whirl of perpetual motion.)

MALCOLM: I've heard George is going to put a question on finance.

ANDREW: Yes, that's right.

MALCOLM: Well we must check, I do need to hear it, so that it's watertight, so there's nothing between us. I want to hear the question before we go in.

*(*ANDREW *looks a little uneasy.)*

ANDREW: Yeah, yeah, he'll come in.

MALCOLM: He's not in his office.

ANDREW: That's right.

MALCOLM: Will he be? George will be available? Well won't he?

*(*MALCOLM *is frowning in evident puzzlement.)*

ANDREW: Malcolm, I'm afraid I have to tell you George is out of control.

*(*MALCOLM *turns at once to his political assistant.)*

BRUCE: There we are.

MALCOLM: I see.

ANDREW: Yeah.

BRUCE: I told you . . .

MALCOLM: You *said*, Bruce, you said you smelt this . . .

BRUCE: Honestly!

*(*ANDREW *is indignant.)*

ANDREW: It's nothing serious. For goodness' sake, he always comes back. Off for some tobacco and then he legged it. *(He turns, opening his arms to him, appealing.)* From what I've heard you're not above legging it yourself . . .

*(*MALCOLM *shifts.)*

MALCOLM: Well . . .

ANDREW: Where did Bruce find you? I heard a video arcade. On the Nintendo machine.

MALCOLM: I'd never seen one before. My children had mentioned it. I was pretty good at it. Wasn't I, Bruce?

BRUCE: Indeed, sir. Very much so.

(*They both smile.*)

MALCOLM: And anyway, I wasn't gone long.

(LINDSAY *is standing waiting to be introduced.*)

LINDSAY: We haven't met.

ANDREW: Oh God, I'm sorry . . .

LINDSAY: My name is Lindsay Fontaine.

ANDREW: I hardly need say, Malcolm Pryce, the Shadow Chancellor . . .

MALCOLM: Yes. How do you do?

(*They shake hands.* ANDREW *smiles, trying to ease things along.*)

ANDREW: Lindsay here is making a submission. To fill the conspicuous vacancy we have.

MALCOLM: Ah yes. Which one is that?

ANDREW: (*Smiles*) Malcolm, we need a new advertising agency. In charge of posters and print.

MALCOLM: Oh yes. I forgot. Didn't the last lot fall down a hole?

(*They both smile, a familiar joke.* LINDSAY *looks between them.*)

LINDSAY: I gather, we've all read, you have had some problems . . .

MALCOLM: You could say.

LINDSAY: Your last agency walked out. Or were sacked. It wasn't quite clear.

ANDREW: It was by mutual agreement. Wasn't it, Malcolm?

MALCOLM: The last words I heard was someone saying 'Throw them to the dogs . . .' (*He smiles amiably.*) Now if that's what you mean by mutual agreement . . .

LINDSAY: Yes. I heard the dog phrase. But someone has to do the job.

MALCOLM: (*Smiles again*) Do they?

LINDSAY: I think so. (*She stops a moment, puzzled.*) You can't fight an election without professional help.

(MALCOLM *looks at her a moment as if there were a great deal he could say, but is choosing not to.*)

MALCOLM: Possibly. You may well be right. I wish you luck.

(*But* LINDSAY *is frowning, not understanding his heavily ironic tone.*)

LINDSAY: But? But what?

MALCOLM: No, nothing.

LINDSAY: What are you saying? Are you against help?

MALCOLM: No, the job must be done. And perhaps it's best you do it . . .

(BRUCE *has been discreetly fretting and now leans in to his ear.*)

BRUCE: Sir, I think we should be going.

MALCOLM: (*To* LINDSAY) Why not? . . . (*To* BRUCE.) All right, I'm coming . . . (*To* LINDSAY *again.*) Andrew will tell you, it's a vexed issue . . . as you say, we've had packaging experts before . . .

BRUCE: You are late for your next meeting . . .

MALCOLM: But some of us – that includes me – believe if your policy is right . . . if it corresponds to people's own experience . . . if it will fulfil a real need in people's lives . . . as I believe ours will, Andrew . . .

ANDREW: No question. No one's questioning that.

MALCOLM: Good. (*His words are suddenly incisive, a real seriousness appearing.*) Then we need not waste time on the design of the envelope, so long as we trust the document inside.

(MALCOLM *stands, his point made, then starts to move.*)

LINDSAY: Yes but . . .

(*And now* GWENDA *comes running back in. The whole lobby is beginning to get much busier.*)

GWENDA: I think we've got good news . . .

LINDSAY: I'm not sure things are that simple . . .

BRUCE: Sir . . .

MALCOLM: I'd love to continue this . . .

BRUCE: Sir . . .

(ANDREW *has headed over in* GWENDA'*s direction.*)

ANDREW: What are you saying, a sighting?

GWENDA: Well someone who looks like him at least.

ANDREW: Thank God. Does he look enough like him to lead at Prime Minister's Question Time?

(*The* POLICE *are now heading down to organize the public into a line which turns a ninety-degree angle at the centre of the lobby.*)

POLICE: Into lines now please, into lines everyone . . .

BRUCE: Sir, we're going this way.

MALCOLM: I'm sorry to leave this . . .

LINDSAY: What you're saying is interesting . . .

ANDREW: Are you going after him?

MALCOLM: I certainly don't wish to be rude . . .

LINDSAY: No.

GWENDA: Yes, hold here, why don't you?

BRUCE: This way sir.

> (GWENDA *has gone off again, apparently having seen* GEORGE. MALCOLM *is also moving off, his minder in tow.*)

MALCOLM: Now tell me, where am I going? What am I doing?

BRUCE: You're meeting some people on the terrace out here.

MALCOLM: What people?

> (*Before they have gone off, from the same direction comes* MARY HOUSEGO. *She backs into the lobby, a tall, nervous woman in her late twenties, in a very short suit and carrying an immense bundle of newspapers under one arm, and a portable phone in her other hand.*)

MARY: Are you looking for George?

ANDREW: Yes.

MARY: (*Still looking off-stage*) He's on his way in.

ANDREW: Thank God for that.

> (ANDREW *goes to call* GWENDA *back from the wrong direction in which she has just gone, while the* POLICE *patrol the public into an orderly dogleg.* MARY *heads back towards where she thinks* GEORGE *is.*)

POLICE: Into lines, please, into lines everyone . . .

ANDREW: Gwenda, Gwenda . . .

> (LINDSAY *is still standing slightly taken aback by* MALCOLM's *hostility.*)

LINDSAY: My goodness!

ANDREW: I know.

LINDSAY: People are so frightened. It isn't *voodoo*, what people like me do . . .

> (ANDREW *looks at her a moment, suddenly giving her his whole attention, as* GWENDA *crosses at the back to follow up* ANDREW's *lead.*)

8

ANDREW: No. No. But you might as well get used to it. We give
you this job, you inherit the storm.
(*He holds a warning finger up silently to her as* GWENDA *reappears. She still has her back to them and is looking off-stage, as
is* MARY *who now also reappears.*)

GWENDA: All right, this is good. Wait. Yes. Yes. Mary?

MARY: I think so. Yes. It's a definite appearance. (*She turns back
and watches again.*) He's coming. This time he's coming.
(*There is a long silence.* LINDSAY, ANDREW *and* MARY *all stand
looking off-stage while the public, waiting for the other moment, is
also silent.*)
Yes. We're bringing him in.
(*There is a much shorter silence and into it walks* GEORGE JONES.
*He is at his most modest and the suit he is wearing is unremarkable.
You would not notice him in a crowd. But the quiet sparkle in his
manner makes it plain he knows the anxiety he has caused by his
absence.*)

GEORGE: Andrew.

ANDREW: George.

GEORGE: Were you looking for me?
(*His tone is gentle and he smiles beatifically.* ANDREW *is quiet too.*)

ANDREW: Where were you?

GEORGE: I was in the park. I went for a walk in the park.

ANDREW: How was it?

GEORGE: Fine. It was like spring. I looked round. People were
walking. And kissing. And talking. I thought, you lucky
people . . . (*He pauses a second.*) You're free and I'm not.
(*Before he can say any more, the* POLICE *call out again and he
reacts at once by heading off briskly towards his office.*)

POLICE: Quiet, please, everyone, silence now please.

GEORGE: Now let me see . . .

POLICE: Quiet in the lobby, please.

ANDREW: George, I wonder, do you have time for a moment with
Lindsay?
(*But* GEORGE *has already got a postcard out of his pocket with a
list of priorities and is moving away with* GWENDA *and* MARY,
talking into the distance. ANDREW *is fighting a losing battle as he
follows.*)

9

GEORGE: Let me see now, I need to talk to Derek. The European group, what's happened to that? Also, I can't leave Michael any longer. And Malcolm, I must see Malcolm before I go into Question Time . . .

GWENDA: Of course.

POLICE: Quiet please!

(*As* ANDREW *disappears with the leader's group, he calls back to* LINDSAY.)

ANDREW: Sorry . . . we will be in touch with you.

POLICE: Absolute silence. Absolute silence in here.

(*There is a moment's pause, then the back doors are flung open. Standing already waiting to pass through the lobby is the* SPEAKER's *procession. A man in full eighteenth-century fig – stockings and knickerbockers – is carrying the mace and behind him the* SPEAKER *himself is bewigged. The* POLICE *have assembled on either side as the procession takes a few steps forward. There is a great cry.*)

CLERK: Speaker!

(*In silence now, the whole group pass through the lobby, the public watching in awe.*)

Hats off, strangers!

(*They pass on through. Before the crowd breaks up,* LINDSAY *turns and looks down towards us. She frowns, obviously puzzled by what she has just seen.*

A bell rings and the crowd disperses.)

SCENE THREE

Now, merging into the previous scene, like a cross-fade, the familiar sound of the House of Commons in uproar. GEORGE *is on his feet across the dispatch box.*

GEORGE: The country reels. The country is tired. This government is tired. It has lived out its life. It has been here too long and now it continues without any vitality or effective policy.

(*From all round him there are cries of 'Question!', 'What's your*

question?')
It exists purely for one purpose: it exists in order to continue
to exist.
(*There is uproar.*)
It feels, it looks, it sounds like a lonely drunk wandering
through the streets at four-thirty in the morning, muttering
to itself, blaming its misfortunes on others and desperately
searching, scrabbling through the early morning trashcans
for any political ideas it might still be able to lift.
(*More cries of 'Question', 'Ask a question'.*)
It falls. It falters. Only power itself motivates it now. The
head has been cut off. But the chicken keeps running. How
long? The honourable members ask me for a question. Yes I
will give them a question. Please. Please tell us how long?

SCENE FOUR

GEORGE *comes cheerfully from the House down the corridor into the
outer room of the Leader of the Opposition's offices. It is cramped and
higgledy-piggledy, piled with newspapers, order papers, files and a
television set and with three hugely cluttered desks set out in the
panelled Gothic room.* GWENDA *is already waiting for him, and gets
up to greet him as soon as he arrives, trailed by* MARY *who, as usual,
is carrying huge quantities of newspapers.*

GEORGE: I know, I know. You don't have to tell me . . .
MARY: On the contrary, no, it was very good . . . perhaps well . . .
     a little long.
GEORGE: Yes. I'm aware.
MARY: Question. You are meant to ask questions.
GEORGE: I know.
     (*He just smiles good-humouredly and stands taking papers from*
     GWENDA.)
GEORGE: Thank you, Gwenda.
MARY: You had them.
GEORGE: I did. And I had Kendrick. He was sweating. I've
     noticed. It's always on his nose. His nose gets wet. Then I

lost him. It was that bloody chicken.

MARY: It doesn't matter.

GWENDA: Will you sign these in here?

(He is already leaning over the side of a desk and signing one letter after another, perhaps fifty in all. A tall, thin man in his forties has come in and put his briefcase down on one of the desks. His name is OLIVER DIX, and he is slightly stooped and gloomy, like a very tall academic.)

MARY: It'll play on the six, you wait, they'll run it.

GEORGE: The bit about the drunk?

MARY: Oh no question, that's the bit. It'll play the six.

GEORGE: Well that's good. Hello Oliver.

OLIVER: George.

GEORGE: *(To GWENDA)* I would love a cigarette.

GWENDA: *(Pleasantly)* Well you can't have one.

MARY: It *will* play the six. *(She turns to OLIVER.)* Don't you think so?

OLIVER: If you say so, Mary.

MARY: To be honest, I'm not sure it's got the legs for the nine.

(GWENDA has gone out, taking the first signature off in a hurry and she passes ANDREW coming into the room with his briefcase and more papers. OLIVER has chosen another desk to perch on and is also now reading documents and making marks down the sides.)

GEORGE: The chicken, you know, I don't know where it came from, I wasn't even thinking . . . Andrew, hello.

ANDREW: Hello George.

OLIVER: I liked the trashcan. The trashcan was good. All that.

GEORGE: It was going well. I know.

ANDREW: *(Fresh to the subject)* Good question, George.

GEORGE: Till the end it was. I couldn't think how to end it.

(GWENDA has come back in with a pile of documents which she puts down beside him, but he takes no notice.)

GWENDA: Can you look at these please, they're for this evening . . .

GEORGE: Actually I know how it happened, I've just realized, I had chicken for lunch.

(He smiles to himself, as everyone else works on.)

ANDREW: George we need to see you.

GEORGE: The word popped up.

ANDREW: Just for a moment.

(ANDREW, *on the edge of the desk is leafing casually now through the documents* GWENDA *brought.*)

GEORGE: What's this? Transport and technology in Europe. I'm not reading this.

OLIVER: (*Without looking up*) We need you to read it.

GEORGE: Don't bog me down in detail. Push the work away. Push it away.

OLIVER: (*Smiles*) There's a fine line, George, between getting bogged down in detail and being inadequately briefed. Which, if you were, would be my fault. (*He gestures humorously round the whole room.*) Or, anyway, *our* fault. (*But* GEORGE *has moved away to where he can stand alone and watch the rest of them working.*)

GEORGE: You can't reach me. No one can reach me. I believe in order and calm.

GWENDA: There's a couple of people waiting in your office. They've been waiting half an hour.

OLIVER: The PLP meeting. Gwenda's got the minutes. Have you seen them?

(GEORGE *just smiles and shakes his head.*)

GWENDA: Hold on, I'll get them back from your desk.

(GEORGE *takes no notice of* GWENDA *as she hurries out but carries on as if continuing his last speech.*)

GEORGE: In Molière, you know – you don't go to the theatre, you're missing out there, everyone in politics should – in Molière it's always the maid I like best. She comes on early, before you meet the mistress. She's always excited because her mistress is going to get laid. What's great is, her mistress doesn't have to get excited. The maid does it for her, you see. (*He suddenly bends at the hip and does a little graceful imitation of a French maid.*) They flick these little aprons, sometimes little feather dusters they have. (*He turns and looks round the room.*) That's you. That's you lot. You're the maids. And you're all of a tizz. And – as in Molière – you're all of a tizz in order that I may be calm.

(GWENDA *has reappeared with the missing papers and put them down on the desk in front of* GEORGE. *The others carry on with their work,* OLIVER *making notes,* MARY *reading newspapers,* ANDREW *now seizing his cue to speak.*)

ANDREW: Right, then, OK . . .

OLIVER: That's us in our place then. Maids!

GEORGE: Get going Andrew.

ANDREW: I met Lindsay Fontaine.

GEORGE: Ah yes. How was she?

ANDREW: Well, that's the whole point. That's what I was wondering. (*He pauses.*) I'm not sure I know what we want.
(OLIVER *has looked up, interested.*)

GEORGE: Go on.

ANDREW: You see, I mean, it's a question of strategy. The election is likely to be some time away. It's November. Kendrick's not going to go before Christmas. Not if he's got any sense . . .
(GWENDA *almost without noticing has got up from* GEORGE'*s desk and moved elsewhere so he can sit and put his legs up.*)
But the fact is, we're well on in our planning. The Strategy Unit is already in place. We have a campaign. We've even fixed slogans.

MARY: (*Smiles*) You're asking do we really need someone creative?

ANDREW: Sort of.

OLIVER: Or shall we have someone who'll do what we say?
(OLIVER *says this drily but* GEORGE *is already probing elsewhere.*)

GEORGE: We're not far down the road with her?

ANDREW: Oh God, no.

GEORGE: How committed is she?

ANDREW: There's no question she's serious.

GEORGE: It was good. It was marvellous.

MARY: She did the nurses. The teachers. Everything she does is first-rate.
(OLIVER *has turned now, his whole attention given to this.*)

OLIVER: She is a Labour Party member?

ANDREW: Yes. Yes. Just.

OLIVER: What do you mean, just?

ANDREW: She only joined ten days ago.

GEORGE: What?

ANDREW: I know but be fair, George. No one's a member. Do you know any members? I mean outside people like us?

OLIVER: Andrew . . .

ANDREW: All right, she joined lately. She didn't get round to it. It's like hang-gliding, or learning a second language. Joining the Labour Party is something people mean to get round to do.

(GEORGE, *his feet still on the desk, smiles expansively.*)

OLIVER: And she has done elections?

ANDREW: Oh sure. She's extremely experienced. She's been involved in campaigns all over the world.

MARY: She did the Sandinistas. In Nicaragua.

OLIVER: That's great. They lost.

ANDREW: I know.

OLIVER: And very unexpectedly. When everyone was certain they'd win.

MARY: She gave all the people T-shirts, that's what I heard. Saying Vote Sandinista.

(OLIVER *at once smiles and shakes his head.*)

OLIVER: And people being what they are, I suppose, they wore her T-shirts in the polling booths while they put their cross the other way.

ANDREW: That's right.

OLIVER: Yeah. I know.

(*They all laugh grimly as* OLIVER *moves through the room suddenly showing some feeling.*)

It's a big disadvantage. If you're a progressive. We're meant to believe in the wisdom of the people. 'The people! The people!' we say. But the truth is, the people do stupid things. Like wear your bloody T-shirt and then vote against you.

GEORGE: It's their right. It's the only right they've got.

(*There is a moment's silence.*)

You can never depend on them.

(GEORGE *looks away, seeming to be thinking of something else entirely. A chill in the room.*)

15

OLIVER: This time we'll be fine.

(GEORGE *turns back to* ANDREW.)

GEORGE: So what are you saying, Andrew? You don't think she's tough enough?

ANDREW: Oh no she's tough.

OLIVER: Then what?

ANDREW: She's win-at-all-costs. She's sell-your-own-mother. That doesn't worry me. (*He looks round a moment.*) It's more . . . I know it sounds silly. She makes me nervous. I don't think we know who she is.

(*The others frown, restless now. But* GEORGE *turns calmly to* GWENDA, *quite level.*)

GEORGE: Give me a cigarette.

OLIVER: Look . . .

GEORGE: I understand.

(GEORGE *smiles, knowing what* ANDREW *means.* GWENDA *has taken one cigarette from a packet and he now plays with it, not lighting it.*)

ANDREW: I suppose . . . I don't know . . . I suppose what I'm saying is, like with Oliver . . . he and I go back a long way. We travelled the same highway. Via student politics. We both ran Students Unions. So we have that. It's solid. And, as we're both always saying, nothing we've encountered in the Labour movement has ever seemed to us one-tenth as bad . . .

(*They all smile at this, but* ANDREW *goes on, serious.*)

And you, George, of course, well I mean obviously, I know your union, I know every official, I know that part of South London, I know every single person who shaped your beliefs. (*He stops, frowning.*) But now, I find more and more when people join us, I think who are these people? Who are they? Really? And so all the time I'm feeling, hold on, look, there's a battle ahead. It's not far away. The most important battle of our lives. To me, now, at this moment, it's all about character. When it comes to it, will they hold up?

(OLIVER *breaks in, impatient now, but trying to keep humorous.*)

OLIVER: I think you're just getting old.

ANDREW: Well possibly.

OLIVER: I think you're threatened. Someone new comes in at this
   stage . . .
ANDREW: Yes of course.
OLIVER: When we've done all the work. In this room. This
   group, together.
ANDREW: I don't want our purposes unbalanced.
OLIVER: (*Smiles*) You mean by someone cleverer than you are?
ANDREW: Thank you.
OLIVER: (*His point proved*) You're threatened!
ANDREW: Well do you think you know who she is?
   (*But* OLIVER *just smiles.*)
OLIVER: Lindsay Fontaine? Sure, I've seen her. I saw her once on
   TV. Lindsay's who people are. These days. That's who
   people are. They're like that.
ANDREW: Meaning?
OLIVER: Professionals. A lot of front maybe. With a lot of
   confidence. Maybe . . . OK . . . underneath a bit lost. Not
   knowing what they think. Used to affluence. And things not
   being difficult. (*He smiles and gestures across the room.*) The
   big difference is: she just hasn't been through it. What
   you're saying is, she hasn't been tempered. Because she
   hasn't been through the abuse.
MARY: No that's right.
OLIVER: She hasn't known what it's like to be powerless. (*He
   picks up the nearest newspaper.*) And take this crap every day.
   Always under fire. As well as from the Party. From your own
   MPs. To the point where you get distrustful. Or chippy. Or
   violent. She comes fresh. Unlike us. (*He looks a moment at*
   ANDREW, *then smiles.*) Well maybe that's an advantage.
   (MARY *looks across at* GEORGE, *like everyone, conscious of his
   silence.*)
MARY: George, you've met her. What do you think of her?
   (GEORGE *pauses a moment.*)
GEORGE: Yes. The problem is recruitment. I understand exactly
   what Andrew means.
   (GWENDA *gets up and leaves the room carrying a pile of mail
   away.*)
   The point is, you see, life's much less tricky for the Tories.

They have the advantage over us. They simply ask, what
school did he go to? What bank did he work in? Is he a QC?
They use all the people who sell each other houses. They give
jobs to the people who sell them their shares. Hell, they have
whole troops of infantry. Who wear the same uniforms. And
gather round flags. Rock-solid infantry, who all understand,
they all understand, the point of it all is one thing. One
objective. Which everyone knows. And is loyal to. (*He smiles
and sits back.*) Money's a simple master in that way. But our
master is different. And causes more argument. Our master
is justice. (*He spreads his hands ironically.*) And no two people
agree what that is.

(OLIVER *is shifting discontentedly wanting to interrupt but*
GEORGE *looks at him before he can.*)

So – yes, you're right – we always have this dilemma. Justice
has no organizations. It has no schools. It did have once.
They were called unions. But the communities that
produced them have gone. The industries have gone. So now
justice recruits from the great deracinated masses. The
people from nowhere. Who have nothing in common.
Except what they say they believe in.

(*There is a silence in the room.* GEORGE *has been playing with
the unlit cigarette, and now he throws it down on the table in
front of him.*)

And that doesn't always end up being enough.

(OLIVER *looks round the room alarmed and searching for
support.*)

OLIVER: Now come on, hold on, I don't like the tone of this . . .
GEORGE: (*Smiles*) Go to the theatre, I keep telling you. Brutus has
    qualms.
OLIVER: What does that mean?
GEORGE: There's a scene in a tent. Before battle. All leaders have
    them. In plays, the leader always has a quiet crisis.
OLIVER: Then? Then what happens?
GEORGE: Oh then. . . .
    (*He smiles, deliberately playful.*)
OLIVER: Come on, tell me. I didn't read English.
    (GEORGE *stirs now, thoughtful.*)

GEORGE: It's all right, Oliver. Then they always murder their
    doubts.
OLIVER: Thank God for that.
    (*They smile, but* ANDREW *is still worried.*)
ANDREW: I couldn't help noticing, Malcolm didn't like her.
GEORGE: (*Looking up*) Malcolm met her?
ANDREW: It was chance. He gave her a hard time.
GEORGE: In what way?
ANDREW: Oh you know he tried the old packaging argument . . .
OLIVER: Oh please!
ANDREW: 'This party doesn't need all these nasty, modern
    techniques . . .'
    (*They all smile.*)
    But underneath . . . I thought it was instinct. He just didn't
    like her.
    (GEORGE *is looking thoughtful but* OLIVER *is impatient.*)
OLIVER: Oh come on, Andrew, it's simpler than that. (*He shakes
    his head.*) He doesn't have to like her. He's the pretender.
    He's the Number Two. It's easy being Malcolm. In
    management studies, we recognize this. He has a classic
    positioning technique. He keeps a nice distance. A well-
    judged distance, from which he raises an eyebrow at
    everything we do. Then when something goes wrong . . . oh
    well, there we are. He isn't implicated. (*He pauses, incisive.*)
    It's textbook Number Two behaviour.
    (GWENDA *has come back into the room and is hovering at the
    door.*)
GWENDA: I'm sorry, George, but they really can't wait any more.
    (GEORGE *gets up, decisive now.*)
GEORGE: All right. I like the sound of her. I'll meet her. Apart
    from anything, we're running out of time. We need someone
    soon.
OLIVER: You mustn't take her just to spite Malcolm.
    (OLIVER *has intended this as a joke, but the atmosphere in the
    room changes.* GEORGE *moves a few paces towards him and
    speaks very quietly.*)
GEORGE: I won't hear a word against Malcolm. Is that
    understood? Not a word. Malcolm's all right.

(*There is a silence.* GEORGE *has not raised his voice, but there is no mistaking the rebuke to* OLIVER. *Then* GEORGE *turns to go out with* GWENDA.)

Look in the diary with Gwenda, then ring Lindsay, Andrew, and fix a time for us to meet.

(*He and* GWENDA *go out.* MARY *and* ANDREW *get on with their work, not wanting to comment on the leader's put-down. There is a heavy silence. Then* OLIVER, *dour, speaks.*)

OLIVER: You all think it's funny. I don't think it's funny, when George has his doubts. I think it's bloody dangerous.

ANDREW: Oliver, really, come on.

(ANDREW *is disbelieving, but* OLIVER's *tone is deadly serious.*)

OLIVER: You should have come to me with the whole advertising question, not flung it straight at George like that.

ANDREW: Oliver, come on. Are you serious?

OLIVER: You know I am. You work to me, Andrew. I'm your immediate boss. You go to George through me. I mean it. We're going to have to tighten up procedures. What happened just now mustn't happen again.

(*There is another silence.* MARY *gathers up a paper and walks silently out of the room, not daring to look at* ANDREW *but with the glimmer of a smile on her face.* OLIVER *looks across the room to* ANDREW, *then speaks, trying to conciliate.*)

You know as well as me, George has one weakness.

(ANDREW *looks at him, non-committal.*)

ANDREW: Yes? What?

OLIVER: He's got a fatal weakness. You know that. He likes to take one step back from things. There's a side of him that likes to step back. It's the bloody theatre. He likes tragedy too much. I don't. To me, tragedy's just a posh word for losing. (*He nods slightly.*) This movement's had enough bloody tragedy. That's why in my book tragedy's out.

ANDREW: OK.

(ANDREW *looks a little doubtfully across the room at* OLIVER.)

OLIVER: He mistakes objectivity for stepping right out of it. He likes taking one step away. But he mustn't. He's got to stay in it. He's got to keep going.

20

(There is a short silence. ANDREW *picks up a paper and makes to go out.* OLIVER *is left alone in the afternoon light.)*
OLIVER: Whatever happens he mustn't step back.

SCENE FIVE

As the light fades on OLIVER *alone,* LINDSAY FONTAINE *appears at the front of the stage and talks to us directly.*

LINDSAY: I joined two days later. I had a short interview. George talked about everything except the actual job. As I remember we talked about why nowadays there are five productions of *Richard III* to every one of *Henry V*.

I delegated everything in my own office. I left a colleague in charge. I took my boyfriend out for a good dinner and told him he'd barely see me for the rest of the year. It's fine, you live with that. He knew that as well. That's the deal. He knew I had a new family. And as soon as I arrived, they opened their arms.

SCENE SIX

Bright morning sunlight. The Leader's offices. At once LINDSAY *turns and goes to her new desk at the centre of the cluttered room.* OLIVER *is already working, pecking away at a laptop computer. But before* LINDSAY *can settle,* MARY *comes running into the room in a state of high excitement.*

MARY: All right, here it is, this is going to be a nightmare . . .
LINDSAY: Why?
MARY: It's the pound.
    *(*OLIVER *sits back at once in horror.)*
OLIVER: Oh no, not the pound.
MARY: The pound. The pound. *(She shouts it at him, semi-humorously, as she heads for her phone.)* The pound's going down again.
OLIVER: Oh no. Shit. *(He suddenly raises his voice, genuinely*

angry.) Shit, I don't believe it.

MARY: Yep.

OLIVER: And of course I suppose it's our fault?

MARY: Yep. There's a new opinion poll. Coming out tomorrow.

OLIVER: This is exactly what I feared . . .

MARY: Here we go.

OLIVER: Only sooner.

(MARY *holds her hand over the receiver.*)

MARY: This one's a big one, six pfennigs against the
Deutschmark, five cents against the dollar . . .

(MARY *turns her back on us, to start talking to a journalist on the
other end.* ANDREW *has come quickly into the room with
briefcase and newspapers and heading straight for his desk.*)

ANDREW: Have you heard? Have you got this? There's a run on
the pound.

OLIVER: I just heard.

ANDREW: It's bad for us, it's a City rumour, no more than that.

OLIVER: Is it true?

ANDREW: I don't know. It's a rumour which puts us six points
ahead. I'm sorry, this couldn't be predicted.

(*He has turned to* LINDSAY *to gesture hopelessly, while at the
same time picking up his phone and dialling.*)

LINDSAY: It's fine, don't worry.

ANDREW: I'm sure he will re-schedule your strategy meeting.
Eventually.

(BRYDEN THOMAS *has come ambling into the room. A big
Welshman, in his sixties, he is powerfully built, in an old-
fashioned thick suit. He is sardonic and completely calm.*
ANDREW *looks across to introduce him to* LINDSAY.)

Lindsay Fontaine, this is Bryden Thomas, the Deputy
Leader.

BRYDEN: How do you do?

LINDSAY: Hello.

BRYDEN: I haven't got a telly and I wanted to watch Malcolm.

(BRYDEN *sits down heavily at the side of the room. Meanwhile*
OLIVER *is standing in the middle of the room, thoughtfully
talking to no one in particular.*)

OLIVER: I hate this situation. Because you can't ever win. (*He has*

22

turned to ANDREW, *who is waiting on his call*.) How did you
hear?

ANDREW: By turning on my car radio. It was me who rang
Malcolm. Can you believe it? No one had told him. His
minder's a prick.

BRYDEN: Which one is that? Malcolm has a lot of them.

MARY: (*Hand over mouthpiece*) The new one. Bruce. The one who
calls him sir.

BRYDEN: 'Sir'! We're not Tories.

ANDREW: (*Hand over mouthpiece*) Malcolm loves that. He read
somewhere that Churchill always surrounded himself with
pencil-thin young men.

OLIVER: When is Malcolm on?

MARY: Straight away. Directly after *Pebble Mill*, he's on every
channel. Breathing reassurance.
(ANDREW *has turned away to brief another journalist on the
phone while* MARY *has finished, turned back and is dialling
again*.)

OLIVER: He's using our script?

MARY: Absolutely. There won't be any problem. He's going to
say steady. You know Malcolm, he has no trouble with that.
He's steadiness itself. He's absolutely groaning with gravitas.
He's going to say 'fiscal' a lot.

OLIVER: He loves saying 'fiscal'.

ANDREW: And 'responsibility'.

OLIVER: I assume he's wearing that suit.

MARY: Yes. And his MCC tie. (*She smiles. Then she nods off-
stage*.) George is changing as well.

LINDSAY: George is?

MARY: George was wearing a polo-neck. It was bad luck.

LINDSAY: George is going on TV?

MARY: He has to. He has to look reassuring. Six Pfennigs against
the Mark and George goes pinstripe at least.
(GEORGE *comes in from his office. He is in a dazzling white shirt
and suit trousers, with the jacket over his arm. He has plainly just
put on the shirt and is now about to deal with the cufflinks*.)

GEORGE: So. It's a poll.

OLIVER: Yes.

GEORGE: What a bloody nonsense!

ANDREW: Nice suit, George.

GEORGE: Why does anyone take any notice of polls? (*He shakes his head.*) We all know, we don't trust polls. Ever. We don't believe in them. They're completely discredited. Now tell me what they're saying.

(OLIVER *holds up six fingers.* GEORGE *replies by putting on an inquiring expression and holding up six himself.* OLIVER *nods.* GEORGE *smiles.*)

BRYDEN: So you see, George, it isn't all bad.

(GEORGE *has put the jacket down and now smiles at* BRYDEN *as he slips his cufflinks in.* GWENDA *has appeared carrying the large book which is the Leader's diary and at once goes to stand beside him, moving things round in it obsessively.*)

GWENDA: George, doing this television, you're forty minutes adrift already. Lunch, George, lunch with this backbench delegation . . .

GEORGE: I have to do that.

GWENDA: The Bulgarian Prime Minister, I've already rung, his office says he can't change his schedule. Something drops out.

(GEORGE *has already wandered away to put his tie on.*)

ANDREW: George, Lindsay was due to have your big image meeting.

(GEORGE *smiles absently at her, his cuffs flapping.*)

GEORGE: No problem, Gwenda will find you a time . . .

(*He does not see* GWENDA *give him a filthy look as he is summoned by* MARY *to watch the TV.* Pebble Mill *is just giving way to the* One O'clock News.)

MARY: Malcolm's coming on now. He's already spoken to the Bundesbank.

GEORGE: Good. In German, I hope. (*He turns smiling to* ANDREW, *ignoring the newsreader on the TV.*) I love speaking German. It's so ridiculous. Do you know what they call a Caesarean over there?

ANDREW: No.

GEORGE: You know, when you're wheeled in on the trolley and the pain is too much, you have to say 'I'm sorry, I can't stand

it any longer. Doctor, doctor, I must have a Kaiserschnitt.'
(*He acts the doctor.*) 'Bad news I'm afraid, she got to have a
Kaiserschnitt . . .' (*He laughs.*) And these people run
Europe.

(BRYDEN *is smiling at the joke, and* GEORGE *just touches him
lightly on the shoulder.*)

GEORGE: You all right, Bryden?

BRYDEN: I need a word about the Parliamentary Party.

GEORGE: Restless?

BRYDEN: Of course.

GEORGE: The Party? Restless? My God, you don't say!

BRYDEN: It gets worse as the economic situation gets worse. The
front bench isn't making the impact it should. And they're
worried we're not listening.

GEORGE: Yeah, yeah . . . well we're not.

(GEORGE *moves away chuckling, his attention on his tie.*
GWENDA *is still poring over the diary, which she now lifts up to
show* GEORGE.)

GWENDA: We lose the education meeting at four-thirty and then,
hey presto, everything moves up.

(MARY *calls out from the TV.*)

MARY: Hold on, he's coming up now . . .

(*Now that* MALCOLM *is on,* GEORGE, *still in his stockinged feet
moves to join* MARY *and* OLIVER *watching the television high at
the back of the room.* BRYDEN *goes on watching from his chair.
We half-hear* MALCOLM's *words on fiscal probity.*)

LINDSAY: I'm sorry. Do you mind if I ask a question?

ANDREW: Please. Go ahead.

(LINDSAY *waits a moment, not speaking until she has*
ANDREW's *attention.*)

Yes?

LINDSAY: Why is George agreeing to be interviewed?

(ANDREW *frowns, but before he can answer* LINDSAY *goes on.*)

Why exactly is George going to speak?

ANDREW: To back up Malcolm.

LINDSAY: Yes. Saying what?

ANDREW: That we're soul of probity. The City has no need to fear
us.

LINDSAY: But surely Malcolm's already saying that.

ANDREW: Yes, but this needs extra authority. This is going to be a very big fall.

(OLIVER *has turned, not all that interested in the TV and frowning at this other conversation.*)

OLIVER: Also, understand. This is a dangerous moment. Unless we're careful, Kendrick and the Tories open up our flank.

LINDSAY: Well of course.

OLIVER: In they go, saying, 'This fall is a whiff, it's just a foretaste . . .'

LINDSAY: Yeah, yeah I get that . . .

(GEORGE *has turned away from the television and is coming back towards them to put on his shoes.*)

GEORGE: He was good, he's keeping it simple . . .

OLIVER: We must kill that suggestion.

LINDSAY: But surely Malcolm's already doing that. Why put George up as well?

(ANDREW *and* OLIVER *both smile.*)

OLIVER: Ah well, you see . . .

ANDREW: There is a special problem.

OLIVER: This is the Labour Party. We all have to say the same thing.

(ANDREW *is smiling and has got out a small bleeper from his pocket.*)

ANDREW: That's why we have a system. These things.

LINDSAY: Can I have a look at that?

(*She takes it from him.*)

ANDREW: Over these things we all read what each other has said. (*He runs his finger along the digital display.*) Look, you see there Malcolm says, 'defend a strong pound in all but exceptional circumstances . . .'

(GEORGE's *attention has turned from his shoes to the group round the bleeper.*)

LINDSAY: So George now says . . .

GEORGE: 'Exceptional circumstances'. Word for word. Then it's watertight.

(BRYDEN *holds his bleeper up from his chair.*)

BRYDEN: Me too.

GEORGE: If Bryden or I use any different words then it's a hostage to fortune. The *Daily Express* says we're split.

LINDSAY: Then why say anything?

(GEORGE *blocks out an imaginary headline*.)

GEORGE: JONES IS SILENT. JONES DOESN'T UNDERSTAND ECONOMICS.

LINDSAY: Yes well maybe. But isn't that a risk you should take?

(OLIVER *begins to stir*.)

OLIVER: Lindsay, the point is – we're a government in waiting. We must be responsible. We must never seem to talk the pound down. It's unpatriotic.

LINDSAY: Of course.

OLIVER: 'The pound is falling! Whoopee!' That's a very bad attitude.

LINDSAY: Of course. I see that.

(*She looks, not giving way*.)

OLIVER: George will tell you. We have all discussed this. We agreed this strategy. Right from the start. To stop the pound falling. At all costs.

LINDSAY: Why? (*She laughs at the absurdity of it*.) I mean, why do something which is simply going to help the Tories?

OLIVER: That's not the point! We have to do it.

LINDSAY: And what's more, something at which you're going to fail. (*She has suddenly got up and is getting a thick document from her briefcase*.) George will speak but the pound won't stop falling.

GEORGE: Won't it?

LINDSAY: Well at least not in my view. (*To* ANDREW *and* OLIVER.) You'll have put George out and he will be seen not to have made a blind bit of difference. (*She turns back to* GEORGE.) All that happens is you speak but you end up looking ineffective. Why not leave that to Malcolm?

BRYDEN: (*From his chair at the side*) I must say that's an attractive idea.

(*They start to laugh at* BRYDEN'*s joke, but* LINDSAY *is now showing the document to* GEORGE *who is watching amused*.)

LINDSAY: The odd thing is, this all confirms something I've already been thinking. I was planning to show you our new market research . . .

OLIVER: Oh no!

LINDSAY: At it happens my firm had commissioned some polls . . .

OLIVER: We have polls.

LINDSAY: I've seen your polls. Frankly, they're rustic. (*She turns some pages of the dossier in his hands.*) Seventy per cent agree with this statement: 'The Labour Party no longer stands for anything distinctive.'

OLIVER: Oh come on, now please!

(ANDREW *smiles across at him, amused at the familiarity of this. But* LINDSAY *is beside* GEORGE *who is frowning at the figures.*)

LINDSAY: The worst effect, you'll see, is on your own standing. Look there . . . These verbals . . . There . . .

OLIVER: This is poison! George, she's feeding you poison.

(OLIVER *is calling from across the room but* GEORGE *just looks up, deflective as ever, amused.*)

GEORGE: God, is this all about me? How frightening!

LINDSAY: Look there, you see . . . you always seem to be backing the government and the public ends up thinking you're weak.

(OLIVER *has moved round the room now to counter her.*)

OLIVER: George, you know full well we can't get into this. We discuss this properly or not at all. These are fundamental questions of policy. And a structure exists for discussing such things. (*He is serious, the shadow of old discussions there between them.*) No one here is frightened of re-opening these questions. Everyone here will change everything they've done. If that's what you want. But not change for change's sake. Not because you're bored, George.

(GEORGE *looks at him a moment as if the charge hits home.*)

Not caprice, George. Not whim.

(*There is a moment's silence. Everyone knows a decisive moment has been reached.* GEORGE *quietly closes the dossier.*)

GEORGE: Thank you Lindsay. I have to go. (*He hands the dossier back to her.*) I'm sure this is good. But I have to do it. The reason is simple. It's what Malcolm wants. (*He smiles, gesturing towards* BRYDEN.)

And Bryden will tell you, politics isn't just about strategy. It's also down to personal relationships. (*He looks down a moment, quiet.*) And what Malcolm wants, I will do.

(MALCOLM *appears at the door,* BRUCE *immediately behind him.*)

GEORGE: Malcolm.

MALCOLM: George.

GEORGE: I watched. You were great. Great stuff.

MALCOLM: Did you hear the words that I used?

(*Anticipating,* MARY *has already handed* GEORGE *a piece of paper with her notes from watching the TV.*)

GEORGE: Yes thank you, I've got them.

(*There is a moment's silence,* MALCOLM *a little puzzled by the strange atmosphere in the room.*)

MALCOLM: Your turn in the chair. If you like, I'll walk with you.

GEORGE: Thank you.

(*Again, there is a slight pause, the tone between the two men formal and polite.* GEORGE *looks round a moment.*)

GEORGE: That would be kind.

MALCOLM: (*Turns back*) Am I all right, Bruce?

BRUCE: I think so. We can give it ten minutes, sir.

(ANDREW *looks across to* OLIVER *and makes a wanking gesture with his hand.* GEORGE *straightens his suit and pats its pockets.*)

GEORGE: All right, everyone? Good, then let's go.

(*He goes straight out of the room followed by* MARY, GWENDA, MALCOLM *and* BRUCE. OLIVER *turns, more relaxed.*)

OLIVER: Well thank God for that, you nearly put him off it.

LINDSAY: (*Shrugs*) It's up to him.

OLIVER: I'll say this for you. I understand why you joined the Party two weeks ago. You're a natural Labour Party member. You just made four enemies in under five minutes. (*He smiles.*) Though even by our standards that is going it some.

ANDREW: I know. She was like a veteran. She brought back memories of the great days.

BRYDEN: Andrew, you're far too young. When I joined, we had people who were so offensive they could dispatch a whole Party Conference to the tea-room.

LINDSAY: Thank you.

ANDREW: Lindsay's obviously picked up her technique from them.

(All this is perfectly good-natured but already OLIVER *has picked up her dossier and is quickly flicking through it.)*

OLIVER: I mean, come on, Lindsay, we're not complete idiots. We've read this sort of stuff. We do it ourselves. *(He holds it open contemptuously at any old page and flicks his hand at its charts.)* Demographics. Statistical breakdowns. They're innately conservative. As well you know. What do they tell you? People want hanging back? That half of them would like to send black people home?

(He smiles and throws the dossier down on the desk. But LINDSAY *is already smiling and shaking her head.)*

LINDSAY: You know it really makes me laugh. You say you respect this kind of work. Yet . . . is it Oliver? . . .

OLIVER: It is.

LINDSAY: I have to tell you, Oliver, your body language is expressing nothing but aggression.

OLIVER: Oh really?

LINDSAY: Oliver, please just look at yourself.

*(*ANDREW *and* BRYDEN *are smiling, enjoying this, as* LINDSAY *goes to pick up the dossier, at once handling it much more considerately.)*

The way you handle this document. You riffle through its pages. Wham! You then throw it down. Do you know what emotion you're exhibiting towards this document? Fear.

OLIVER: It isn't fear. It's boredom.

LINDSAY: You don't want to hear what it's saying. Because you're so isolated.

*(*OLIVER *is shaking his head.)*

ANDREW: George isn't isolated. That's the one thing he isn't. He's back in his constituency every weekend. Do you think he doesn't know what people are thinking?

(At the other side of the room BRYDEN *stirs.)*

BRYDEN: It is so, my dear. It's meant to be my job to tell him what's going on out there, to report from the country, from the Party as well . . .

ANDREW: That's right.

BRYDEN: Most times I don't have to. He's way ahead of me. His
instinct is brilliant.

LINDSAY: Then why are you still failing to get him across?

(OLIVER *stands, impatient now.*)

OLIVER: All right, for goodness sake we know there's a problem
of public Perception.

LINDSAY: Perception? There is. (*She opens the dossier again.*)
Seventy-one for 'too thoughtful'. Fifty-five 'downbeat'.
Sixty-four, the killer word. 'Solitary'.

(BRYDEN *smiles and speaks with a deadly sort of quiet.*)

BRYDEN: What would you like? That we all find him a wife?

(*The group look round smiling, glad of* BRYDEN's *intervention.*)

LINDSAY: No.

(*And now* OLIVER *is moving in on her, already putting the next
argument.*)

OLIVER: You ask me why George is doing this interview. It does
him good, that's the point. To appear close to Malcolm.
Malcolm's proximity is very good news. Because Malcolm is
. . . let us say . . . unarguably clever. I don't just mean
clever. I mean Oxbridge. Incisive.

LINDSAY: And George isn't?

(OLIVER *inclines his head, as if cornered.*)

OLIVER: No. Not at all. George is extraordinary. Incorruptible.
A great Party leader. As great in his way as any this Party
has had. And what's more, still full of ideas. But – if we
must identify a political weakness – he cannot in public
always give those ideas articulate expression. (*He pauses,
tightrope-walking.*) So we have sought to take this into
account.

(BRYDEN *is watching silently, giving nothing away.*)

We keep George moving. We brief very hard. He learns his
lines and he sticks to them.

ANDREW: He has to.

OLIVER: This has been the whole direction of this office. Games
theory! If you don't take risks, then you don't make
mistakes.

(LINDSAY *looks round, puzzled.*)

LINDSAY: Yes, I see.

OLIVER: The great thing with George is he knows he has weaknesses. He wants to get better. He wants to improve.

LINDSAY: Well, that's good.

OLIVER: We made a list, early on, of all his worst failings. Each separate failing we put on a card.

ANDREW: (*Smiles*) Colour-coded.

LINDSAY: I'm sure he was grateful.

OLIVER: Then we presented them to him. In a real, late-night brainstorming session. White-knuckle stuff.

ANDREW: It was actually wonderful.

OLIVER: Because he's so eager to learn. (*He smiles.*) We said, let's face it: Card Number One. You do have a problem. With actual consequential factual coherence. You have that problem. You do.

LINDSAY: I see. (*She frowns a moment.*) Is that his worst problem?

OLIVER: Truthfully? (*He waits a second.*) No. No. Card Number Two. You also have problems with judging your length. (ANDREW *nods darkly.*)

ANDREW: Very grave problems.

LINDSAY: Yes, well, I remember. The well-known incident. The Linus Frank programme . . .

OLIVER: It plays in my nightmares.

LINDSAY: I must say, they never stop running it. I saw it last month . . .

OLIVER: (*Shaking his head*) They are such bastards. (*He turns, wounded at the injustice of it.*)

OLIVER: And yet it happened five years ago.

ANDREW: Frank rattled him.

LINDSAY: It *is* very funny. He appears not to understand his own Party's social security policy. He then tries to backtrack. Interminably.

(OLIVER *leans forward, insistent.*)

OLIVER: Lindsay, we could not let that happen again.

ANDREW: We had to deal with this problem. We had to.

OLIVER: That's right. We had to get a check on his flow. We used certain techniques – Bryden knows of them – to tether

32

the balloon under canvas. And then to keep it there.
(LINDSAY *looks sidelong to* BRYDEN *to check his reaction, but he is still impassive.*)
And now we feel they're beginning to work.
(LINDSAY *looks at him sceptically.*)

LINDSAY: You do?

OLIVER: Yes. He's not fouling up.

ANDREW: (*Confirming it*) He's not.

OLIVER: There hasn't been a verbal alert in six months.

LINDSAY: He doesn't foul up. I agree with you. No. But also –
you do have to deal with this – the problem is he doesn't
break through. (*Before they can come back at her, she suddenly
points to the dossier and raises her voice.*) Forty-eight 'boring'.
Thirty-four 'unconvincing'. And thirty-two who just wish
he'd shut up.
(*Suddenly* BRYDEN *stirs himself massively at the side of the
room.*)

BRYDEN: I can't hear this. I really won't hear it. You're talking
about a Party which never wins an election. It loses. And
loses. Time after time. Can you imagine the pressure, the
pressure on the leader as he's brought one thousand different
remedies, each one conflicting, from well-meaning people
who want to see the Party get back? (*He pauses.*) And now
. . . and now when, thanks to him, the moment is coming . . .
the policies are finally in place, the party has been quietened,
essential discipline imposed, then I think Miss Fontaine:
he's brought us this far, so maybe the best thing is we all now
leave him alone. He's decent. He has total integrity.
Underneath his manner, he works like no man I've seen. His
authority stems from his personal character. He's unspoilt.
And in my experience, that's well-nigh unique. (*He shrugs
slightly.*) There's a case against George. Of course. There's a
case against all of us. The Tory Party makes that case every
day. So do its spaniels in the Press. We have no duty to make
it. On the contrary. (*He turns, overwhelmed by feeling.*) I feel
disloyal even talking like this.
(BRYDEN'*s feelings are so obviously real that* LINDSAY *only
joins back in very quietly.*)

LINDSAY: Yes. I understand your feelings. I respect everything you say. But there's an irony here. (*She looks down as if reluctant.*) George is the man who made victory possible. But unless we do something quickly, he's the only thing standing in victory's way.

(*At this, on cue,* GEORGE *opens the door of the room. He stands a moment, quite still and everyone is taken aback to find the man they have been talking about among them.*)

OLIVER: George . . .

(*He frowns, bemused by* GEORGE's *stillness.*) How was it?

GEORGE: Oh. Well, it was fine.

OLIVER: What happened?

(GEORGE *stands a moment, disturbed.*)

GEORGE: Well of course they said, so you support the government? I couldn't say yes. And of course also . . . I suppose I couldn't wholly say no.

(LINDSAY *is sitting quietly at the side of the room, not looking at* GEORGE.)

OLIVER: So what did you do?

GEORGE: I suppose I flannelled. Yes, I . . . what's the word? . . .

(*He just stops dead, saying nothing.* OLIVER *frowns.*)

OLIVER: What? What is it?

LINDSAY: Rambled?

(GEORGE *looks at her a moment.*)

GEORGE: Yes. Yes, exactly, Lindsay. I rambled. As you had said that I would.

(*There is a moment's pause, then through the door comes* TREVOR AVERY *who is black, in his early thirties and very powerfully built, in a lightweight suit.*)

ANDREW: Yes?

TREVOR: Excuse me, my name is Avery . . .

(ANDREW *frowns.*)

ANDREW: Hold on, have we met before?

TREVOR: Yeah, I'm from Special Branch.

ANDREW: Special Branch? (*He turns in sudden panic.*) Oliver . . .

TREVOR: Oh God, don't say nobody's rung you . . .

OLIVER: Special Branch?

(*Suddenly everyone in the room is having the same thought.*)

34

George, I don't believe it. It can't be. God almighty, the guns
have arrived.

(*Before anyone can react,* MARY *comes running into the room,
breathless.*)

MARY: He's got into a car.

OLIVER: What do you mean? Who has?

MARY: Kendrick.

ANDREW: Kendrick?

MARY: Yes. A journalist rang me. He's been seen. He's going
down the Mall.

(*They all look round, bewildered.*)

ANDREW: Kendrick?

MARY: He's going to the Palace.

ANDREW: He can't be. It's Monday. It's two-fifteen.

(OLIVER *stands completely bemused in the middle of the room.*)

OLIVER: What? *What?* (*Then he turns to* MARY.) A journalist rang
you?

MARY: Number Ten is briefing, there must be an end to
uncertainty.

(GEORGE *starts to nod his head and move away as if this is just
typical.*)

The economy cannot be damaged any further, that's what he
says. The only way of ending the uncertainty is . . .

ANDREW: I simply don't believe it. Now? Today?

OLIVER: What's he up to? He's going before Christmas. What
does he know that we don't?

(*The phones have all started ringing and now* MALCOLM *comes
quickly into the room, followed by* BRUCE.)

MALCOLM: Have you heard this?

BRYDEN: We've heard it.

MALCOLM: The bastard's going down the Mall.

(MALCOLM *turns in despair but* MARY, ANDREW *and* OLIVER
are already answering phones. GWENDA *hurries in carrying the
diary in her hand and poring over it already.*)

MALCOLM: Why didn't we know? Why didn't we know this?

GWENDA: Well, frankly, bang goes the Bulgarian Prime Minister.

OLIVER: (*Hand over phone*) Why's he going when he's six points
behind?

(BRYDEN *has moved across to speak to* GEORGE, *as with her free hand* MARY *reaches to turn up the television, where a* COMMENTATOR *is describing a car approaching the Palace.*)

BRYDEN: George, were you expecting this?

GEORGE: Of course not. No. I'd booked for *Hamlet* this evening. (*He hits the edge of the desk in frustration.*) Oh bugger Kendrick, I really wanted to go.

TREVOR: We do need to have a conference about Mr Jones' protection . . .

MARY: Hold on a moment . . .

(*But* GEORGE *is nowhere near them, still in a world of his own.*)

GEORGE: He does it to annoy me, he knows, he *knows* I'd been looking forward to it all week.

(*The others are all on different phones, talking away about how ready the Labour Party is for the fight.*)

MALCOLM: Aren't they meant to warn us? I thought they're meant to let us have advance notice?

(*But* OLIVER *is turning already to the others, with his hand over the phone.*)

OLIVER: Is there a date? We haven't got a date yet?

ANDREW: (*Hand over phone*) Over here they want to know if George is going to speak.

OLIVER: (*Hand over phone*) Of course he's going to speak. He's got to.

MARY: George is going to go live. The only question is where.

(TREVOR *is shifting uneasily.* ANDREW *is flicking through a desk diary.*)

ANDREW: (*Hand over phone*) It's got to be December 6. Yes, that's right. Hold on. Yeah it's got to be.

MARY: If he's going to speak, I don't want him to do it in here.

(MALCOLM *suddenly loses his temper because no one is taking any notice of him.*)

MALCOLM: For God's sake, we should have *known*. Why didn't we *know*?

ANDREW: Because we weren't watching CEEFAX, it's as simple as that.

(*Suddenly* GEORGE *lifts his arms to the skies and dances.*)

36

GEORGE: Oh God, let it come, yes, let it come, let it come now. Please God, let it come.

(*But everyone is turned away, and nobody notices.*)

MARY: This is a potential Prime Minister . . .

ANDREW: (*Into phone*) Come on you bloody tosspots, where are you . . .?

MARY: He mustn't talk standing up. Standing up is weak.

ANDREW: Does anyone do *anything* down at Walworth Road?

MARY: If he's a Prime Minister, he has to be seen behind a desk.

(*At this moment simultaneous conversations start all over the stage. ANDREW starts yelling at a Labour Party press officer. OLIVER is briefing a journalist. MARY and TREVOR fall into a security discussion. BRYDEN is on another phone spreading the news. Everyone ignores GEORGE who is all by himself. He suddenly smiles at MALCOLM.*)

GEORGE: Well this is what we've been waiting for.

MALCOLM: Yes. Yes it is.

(*The two men stand uncertain a moment. Then they fall into each others' arms, embracing.*)

GEORGE: Good luck, Malcolm.

MALCOLM: Good luck yourself.

(*They stand a moment, quite still in the engulfing chaos, looking into one another's eyes.*)

SCENE SEVEN

The Prime Minister, CHARLES KENDRICK *has walked across Downing Street towards a circle of journalists, cameramen and supporters. A microphone has been set up rather oddly in the street.* KENDRICK *is large and easy-going, and his delivery is not marked with self-doubt. Beside him, a Knightsbridge ash-blonde called* CAROLE.

KENDRICK: This, I know, is a brave decision. It's not one I have taken lightly at all. It is not in any sense impetuous. Because, on the contrary, it is taken to avoid a most damaging risk. We cannot have prosperity, we cannot have

37

sound financial practice until the danger – however remote –
of a possible Labour government is removed from the back of
people's minds.

I would not allow a creeping paralysis to undermine the very
real strides of progress we have made.

I will fight this election – alongside my wife Carole – because I
am tired of the relentless negativity, of listening to an
Opposition which does nothing but run Britain down. That
tires me. Because this is a great country. I believe, the greatest
on earth. So for my children, and their future children – as
well as my wife, Carole – let us end the uncertainty now.

SCENE EIGHT

GEORGE's *flat in Kennington. It is in a fairly anonymous modern
style, in a contemporary block of flats, but one large wall is completely
covered in books. He has a large table which is groaning with piles of
books and papers and at which he is now sitting under an anglepoise,
writing in longhand. It is clear that it is very late at night.* GWENDA *is
sitting well to one side, also working silently, by herself.* LINDSAY
*appears from the kitchen. She is very relaxed and is carrying a carton
of eggs.*

LINDSAY: How do you like them?
GEORGE: I like them scrambled.
LINDSAY: Good.
    (*She puts the eggs down and goes back into the kitchen, as he sits
    back from his desk and talks to her in the other room.*)
GEORGE: Ah yes! Scrambled eggs! When I go to a diplomatic
    banquet, I don't even eat, I sit and I think, I'll be home in an
    hour. And I'll be eating scrambled eggs. (*He smiles
    contentedly.*) I like them with chilli peppers and cream.
    (*Coming back into the room with a bowl and fork which she sets
    down on his desk,* LINDSAY *gives him a frown of disapproval.*)
LINDSAY: Well . . .
GEORGE: I know! It's a position I can't defend in public.
LINDSAY: It's not Party policy?

38

GEORGE: I even cook them with onions. (*He nods at her distaste, then becomes thoughtful.*) I know. But in private . . . it's what I like.

(*She cracks eggs into the bowl and starts to whisk.*)

LINDSAY: Did you know this was coming?

GEORGE: What?

LINDSAY: The election. So suddenly.

(GEORGE *at once smiles.*)

GEORGE: Whatever happens, politicians always say they welcome it. Everything that happens, we pretend it's what we foresaw. It's why I dislike us. The job's inherently undignified.

(LINDSAY *stops and looks at him a moment.*)

We have to pretend that we're in control.

(*She frowns and goes back to beating the egg mixture with a fork. He looks thoughtful at what she's doing.*)

LINDSAY: I was surprised he could do it. Constitutionally.

GEORGE: Ah.

LINDSAY: I mean, go for an election without letting you know.

(*He smiles, his point made.*)

GEORGE: That's what I mean. There is no constitution. It's one of those words which Kendrick will use. It means 'doing what I want to'. But saying 'constitution' makes him feel big.

(LINDSAY *smiles at this.*)

I've watched him. 'Massive troop movements'. That's another favourite of his. He'll comment on any war. Anywhere. However obscure. I think, why's he making a statement about some piddling little country ten thousand miles away? And then he'll say, 'Overnight there have been massive troop movements.' He loves them. (*He laughs, happy.*) After a while, you notice these things.

(LINDSAY *looks across, quiet.*)

LINDSAY: What's he like? Do you like him?

GEORGE: He's room temperature. He's nothing more.

(*The remark is casually made, but he's thoughtful again.*)

LINDSAY: Andrew said to me, don't be deceived by George. Underneath, you're as tough as they come.

GEORGE: Ah.

LINDSAY: He told me to watch you during the Cenotaph ceremony. You love it, he said.

GEORGE: Yes. Yes I do.

LINDSAY: 'It's the highlight of his year, because he's surrounded by military.' I must admit that did make me laugh.

GEORGE: Why?

LINDSAY: Because that's my own background. The Army, I mean. I was brought up in Germany. My father's still there today.

(GEORGE *smiles*.)

Then I thought, yes, of course George likes the Army. For the same reasons I did. Eventually.

GEORGE: Yes. I'm afraid there's a sense in which I even quite like a war.

LINDSAY: I see that. The country all pulls together. 'People do what needs to be done . . .'

(*They both smile at this obvious quotation from* GEORGE.)

You have a lot of friends in the Army?

(*He looks at her thoughtfully.*)

GEORGE: I think they know I'd pull the trigger. In a fifty-fifty, I could do the deed. And then I'd be able to live with it. (*He leans back a moment, thoughtful.*) That's something they understand. (*He puts down his paperwork.*) I've moved three streets. In my whole lifetime. Remember. I was born in Kennington, just three streets away. My father's still there. Right by the Granada. And in fifty years I've moved four hundred yards. I'm stubborn. I've denied myself everything. (*He is quite still.*) It would hardly be worth it. To have sacrificed everything. If at the end you were just going to lose.

(*He thinks a moment.*)

LINDSAY: And will you beat him?

GEORGE: Yes. Yes, absolutely.

LINDSAY: Are you sure?

GEORGE: Yes. Oh yes indeed.

(*Suddenly through the door come the rest of the group who have let themselves in.* OLIVER, MARY *and* ANDREW *are all soaked*

40

through and are taking off their wet coats. They also put
supermarket bags down on the main table in the room.)

GEORGE: Andrew, my goodness . . .

ANDREW: I know.

GEORGE: You're drenched.

OLIVER: We all are.

MARY: It's hell out there.

ANDREW: It's murder. And my God, just guess where we've been!

(ANDREW *turns grinning with a big supermarket bag in his hand.*
Everyone is settling in as if for a known ritual: the team meeting.
OLIVER *is getting beer out of the supermarket bags,* MARY *starts*
unpacking food. GWENDA *smiles at them and continues working.*
GEORGE *wanders away amused at how they're taking his place*
over.)

GEORGE: I've no idea. Where have you been?

OLIVER: Visiting the Woodentops.

(MARY *is standing directly opposite* LINDSAY *and holding up a*
carton of eggs she has got out of the bag. She's a little embarrassed.)

MARY: Oh Lord, I brought eggs as well.

(OLIVER *snaps open a beer and smiles.*)

OLIVER: You should have been there. At Party Headquarters. You
would have loved it.

GEORGE: Would I?

ANDREW: This Party does have a genius for containing its
excitement.

OLIVER: My God! Dozy isn't the word.

(*They all laugh, high as kites,* MARY *automatically getting cutlery*
from the kitchen, as ANDREW *stands in the middle of the room and*
acts out the scene.)

ANDREW: 'This is it! This is the moment! This is what we've been
waiting for! At last it's arrived.' Derek. Secretary of the Party.
Gold glasses. Ballpoints on parade. Here. (*He points to his top*
pocket.) Deep bureaucratic frown. Woodentop horror. 'Does
this mean I can't take my leave?'

(*They all laugh,* MARY *coming back in, laying the table for a*
meal.)

MARY: That isn't fair. I'm just as bad. I was going on a bicycling
holiday in Ireland.

ANDREW: Oh really?

MARY: Sure. With some old friends from school. Girlfriends.
(Everyone stops a moment, a little bit taken aback by this revelation.)

GEORGE: Goodness.

ANDREW: You still have a private life?

MARY: Yes. *(She blushes, rather embarrassed.)* I mean, well, yes. Of a kind.
(She resumes laying the table. ANDREW and OLIVER are clearing it of papers and books. LINDSAY just watches.)

OLIVER: It's all right. No need to be embarrassed. Andrew's just jealous.

ANDREW: I am. I can't remember when I last saw my children.

OLIVER: Mine send me polaroids. It's very good of them. That way I can watch them grow up.
(GEORGE is standing, frowning.)

GEORGE: I thought Malcolm was joining us.

OLIVER: Yes he was going to.

GEORGE: But?

OLIVER: He just rang.
(There is a slight pause.)
He said you should go ahead. It's your show. He doesn't feel he should interfere.

GEORGE: Interfere? He won't come and be part of this?

OLIVER: Well no.
(There is a slight silence, OLIVER refusing to say more. MARY automatically takes the bowl of eggs from LINDSAY. GEORGE, by himself, nods.)

GEORGE: Uh-huh.

MARY: I'll take those.

ANDREW: Now shall we have a look at this thing?
(From the supermarket bag he has taken out a huge ring-binder, pristine, enormous, which he now opens. GWENDA has got up to join them.)
Fresh from Mount Ararat. Written in stone. The war book. The whole campaign mapped out, charted and cross-indexed . . .

GEORGE: Well done, Andrew.

ANDREW: No, it was Gwenda.

GWENDA: Not really.

ANDREW: Well then, the two of us. We work as a team.
(*He makes a small move to hug her, but, embarrassed, she is already handing everyone sheaves of paper.*)

GWENDA: This is the digest. You'll see if you look, the plan is like last time, each morning's press conference establishes a theme . . .

GEORGE: We can see. Tuesday health, Wednesday education, Thursday health . . .

GWENDA: (*Smiles*) Friday health . . .

GEORGE: Lord, do we ever do anything else?
(*They are all wandering round, engrossed in their copies.*)

OLIVER: I know but it's right. There's no question. Health is the lever. Health is the key. Health is the knife that's going to detach voters from their primary loyalties and get them churning . . .

GEORGE: Ah yes, 'churning'! I'd forgotten . . .

OLIVER: It'll get them moving our way.
(ANDREW *is gesturing at the book.*)

ANDREW: Everything's here. The list of key campaigners. When they speak. When they move. An appendix of bull points. Notes on vocabulary. All the words we can't use.

LINDSAY: I like this one. 'Never use the word equality. The preferred term is fairness.'

OLIVER: I know. But it's right. It's been tested. Everyone's in favour of fairness. But equality . . . no. That puts people off.
(MARY, *laying the table, has picked up one of the schedules and is frowning at it.*)

MARY: I'm sorry, you know, I mean I'm just thinking . . . looking at it now, in cold print . . .
(ANDREW *looks up, anticipating from her tone.*)

ANDREW: Yes?

MARY: I suppose I'm just asking . . . we are *sure*, aren't we? I mean, is it right to get off the economy quite as soon as we do?
(*At once* OLIVER *and* ANDREW *come pounding in on her.*)

OLIVER: Oh God!

ANDREW: Now look . . .

OLIVER: Oh come on now, Mary . . .

MARY: All right, I know! I do know . . .

(*She puts up her hands protectively.*)

OLIVER: We have been through this so many times. Finally the
economy is always going to be a Tory issue. It's theirs. They
own it. However unfair it is. I wish it weren't so. But it's true.

(*Before* MARY *can interrupt he comes in again strong.*)

OLIVER: And let's not embark on any stupid fantasies. Because
that is not something we can change in the space of three
weeks.

ANDREW: (*Writing now*) It's not.

OLIVER: George can speak all he likes on the caring issues. Health.
Education. He plays to his pluses, that's fine. What he
mustn't do is in any way remind people that when he's elected
he's going to be in charge of their money. Because that's where
people don't trust him at all.

GEORGE: It's true.

(GEORGE *smiles self-deprecatingly.*)

MARY: I know, all right, I know that's the theory . . .

OLIVER: It's more than a *theory*.

MARY: Are we saying we can't mention the economy at all?

OLIVER: No. Of course not. We mention it. Often.

ANDREW: Then we move off it.

(*They smile, but then* OLIVER *suddenly raises his voice.*)

OLIVER: Mary, there are no votes for us there.

(*She looks at him doubtfully.*)

For God's sake, Mary we do have to be disciplined. If you
want to know the truth, the economy's stuffed. It's totally
buggered. We've seen the official Treasury figures – the real
ones, unfiddled, uncensored – and they are far worse than
anyone will ever let on.

GEORGE: They are. They're frightening.

OLIVER: And yet . . . you know . . . it drives you mad with
frustration. You want to proclaim this fact from the roof. And
you can't. Why not?

(MARY *waves a hand, giving in.*)

MARY: All right, I know . . .

OLIVER: Because the one thing we're sure of, from every single survey we do: people run back to Nanny. The worse things are, the more likely they are to vote Tory. They only vote Labour when they think they can afford to.

(MARY *resumes laying the table*.)

MARY: All right. You're right. I'm sorry I mentioned it.

OLIVER: No. I know. But there is here a compelling electoral logic which we ignore at our cost.

(*He is emphatic, but* LINDSAY *is sitting at the side of the room, frowning*.)

LINDSAY: I can see it's tough. I do see the problem. But if the economy really is in this terrible state . . . I mean what will we do?

OLIVER: Do?

LINDSAY: Yes. When we get into power?

(OLIVER *looks across at* GEORGE.)

GEORGE: By all means. She's got to know sometime.

(*There is a moment. Then* OLIVER *speaks, the gaiety gone now and extreme care replacing it*.)

OLIVER: We will abolish mortgage tax relief on our first day in Downing Street.

GEORGE: That's right.

OLIVER: To finance our spending plans.

LINDSAY: I see. (*There is a short silence while she thinks through the implications of this admission*.) So that's how you'll do it.

(OLIVER *smiles and* MARY *reappears from the kitchen having heard all this to put down plates*.)

OLIVER: But this is not something which we can say.

LINDSAY: No.

MARY: Because it's too dangerous. That's putting it mildly. Mortgage tax relief is the homeowner's perk. It's unearned, it's inequitable, it grossly favours the propertied class. In the name of common fairness it should be withdrawn.

(OLIVER *smiles at this homily*.)

OLIVER: Yes, thank you, Mary.

MARY: But sadly, saying so is not voter-friendly. Because homeowners do not quite see it this way.

(GEORGE *sits back in his chair.*)

GEORGE: We did consider announcing it.

OLIVER: Yeah. At length.

GEORGE: In Shadow Cabinet.

OLIVER: But George ruled against it. As he did against announcing certain other proposals. Which, God willing, he *will* implement. But which for the moment would be . . . (*He pauses, the tactician.*) . . . well, too great a struggle to communicate. In the short term they'd be vote-losing positions. (*He shrugs.*) So we cannot put pieces down on those squares . . .

GEORGE: That's right.

(*Pleased with his own logic,* OLIVER *now gets up, a drink in his hand and expands on the subject which means most to him, as* MARY *goes out again.*)

OLIVER: Elections, you see, people think they're about arguments . . .

(ANDREW *shakes his head at the absurdity of this idea.*)

They think when politicians speak it's an act of sense. But it's not. It's an act of strategy. It's taking up a position. It isn't like debate. We're not actually debating.

ANDREW: Far from it.

OLIVER: The only true analogy is with waging war.

(*He cracks open another beer excited, as they go into a self-supporting ritual, repeating the rules of the game.*)

ANDREW: Keep it tight . . .

OLIVER: Yeah . . .

ANDREW: Keep it focused.

OLIVER: Yeah . . .

ANDREW: Keep it on track. Hit hard. Hit constantly. Give them a good pounding.

MARY: Don't get distracted.

ANDREW: Never respond. Never let them set the agenda. And get off their ground as soon as you can.

(MARY *laughs and goes out again.* LINDSAY *looks across to* GEORGE *who, like* GWENDA, *has quietly resumed his work during this.*)

LINDSAY: I see what you're saying. Believe me, I see its

advantages. We all hate danger. Things spinning out of
control. But there is the problem, you have to say the same
things . . .

OLIVER: (*Smiles*) Yip. Over and over.

LINDSAY: You can only use certain subjects . . .

ANDREW: That's right. It's essential.

LINDSAY: And even on those you can't really let go . . . (*She
frowns, starting to move round the room and working it out as
she goes.*) A tight fight, two bodies locked, no big punches,
just slugging it out . . . well yes, electorally it's safe.
(*There is a pause.*)
But it doesn't help George.
(*There is another second's pause. Then* GEORGE *looks up.*)
Doesn't this strategy make George very boring?
(*They all smile and* MARY *returns.*)

OLIVER: It does. Oh indeed it does.

GEORGE: You noticed?
(*He smiles at the others.*)
I'm afraid she's got it in one.
(MARY *smiles at him and touches his arm affectionately.*)

MARY: And you do it very well.

GEORGE: Well bless you. (*He looks ironically at* LINDSAY.) It's
true. Do you think I'm not aware of it? My God, if you
think it's boring for you! Please! Try being me!

OLIVER: George spends his life inside a corset.

GEORGE: And all the time these guys are tightening the
strings . . .
(ANDREW *who has sat down at the table to work on his charts
joins in the common laughter.*)

ANDREW: That's our job!

LINDSAY: And how does that feel?

GEORGE: *Feel?*

LINDSAY: No really. I'm asking.
(OLIVER *and* ANDREW *look up a moment. A sudden pause.*)

GEORGE: Lindsay, for goodness sake, this is my burden. Like
Pilgrim, this is the course I am on. (*He is suddenly firm.*)
You can never let go. You can never lose sight of the
problem that when this Party fell into my hands, it was

torn, disfigured, unelectable. With a matchless capacity for meaningless squabbles and fights. So changing that culture, changing that disastrous habit of anarchy, controlling the Party, getting it to speak with one voice, this has been my historical legacy. Meaning: something I had to do. (*He nods and looks at her.*) I had to make this Party respectable.

(MARY *has appeared silently with a huge tray of food. Eggs for everyone with buttered toast and steaming mugs of milky drinks. She stops a moment.*)

Of course it would be nice – any leader dreams of this – to have thrived in circumstances quite other than the ones I describe. But a politician can only deal with his inheritance. With the situation as it arrives.

(MARY *smiles and sets down the food.*)

MARY: George . . .

ANDREW: Ah eggs!

GEORGE: To tell the truth even . . . that would be wonderful. If words were only their meaning. Well then . . . (*He stops, smiling.*) But words are their effect also.

(*He stands a moment, lost in thought, while* MARY *hands plates out in silence.* ANDREW *has already sat down to fork eggs into his mouth. After a few moments he looks up.*)

GWENDA: George, do you know that you're missing out?

MARY: You are.

ANDREW: These eggs are wonderful.

(*He reaches for a steaming mug from the tray as* OLIVER *sits down next to him and* MARY *beckons* LINDSAY *and* GWENDA *towards the table.* GEORGE *walks round laughing and looking at his watch.*)

ANDREW: What a life! And the Horlicks . . .

GEORGE: Oh God, it's one of those two o'clock meals . . .

(*They all laugh, as they sit down, only* GEORGE *remaining standing behind them.*)

MARY: Certainly. That's why I made Horlicks . . .

GEORGE: Do you remember? Last time . . .

OLIVER: That's right . . .

GEORGE: Where was it?

MARY: Preston.

ANDREW: Preston! Those sausages! Those beans!

GEORGE: Last time, yes? I'll never forget it. It was the last night of the campaign.

MARY: I knew you'd remember the Horlicks.

GEORGE: At four-thirty, totally exhausted . . .

MARY: Andrew fell asleep.

ANDREW: I knew you'd say that.

GEORGE: And I ate his beans. Every one of them.

ANDREW: I woke. No beans.

GEORGE: Those beans, I'd say, were the best of my life.

> (*They all laugh and have all sat down round the table except for* GEORGE *who stands looking affectionately at them all.* LINDSAY *looks up for permission.*)

Eat! Eat! (*He stands a moment watching them all.*) You see in opposition you're always waiting. You go into politics to get something done. And in opposition you do precisely nothing. (*He smiles.*) But for these three weeks at least you exist.

OLIVER: Yes that's right.

> (MARY *looks up, moved by him. She reaches for her mug.*)

MARY: A toast.

> (*They all pick up their mugs.*)

To Pilgrim!

ALL: To Pilgrim!

> (*They all drink.*)

LINDSAY: To Pilgrim. May he win through!

> (GEORGE *takes the chair at the head of the table. Then he takes the hands of* MARY *and* OLIVER *beside him and holds them a moment affectionately. Then he starts to eat.*)

SCENE NINE

The stage becomes much larger. We are in a huge area which has been hired to become the Labour Party Campaign Headquarters. At the back, turned away from us, is the public space where the press conferences will take place. In the distance we can see a huge grey wall, which is currently being hung with enormous red letters. Men on

49

ladders are only half-way through the job, and they continue with it through the next two scenes. It looks very precarious. The half-finished message currently reads IT'S YO LABO PAR.
Meanwhile in the enormous vacant backstage area, there is almost nothing yet except the odd desk and computer terminal, dotted about. There are loads of cardboard boxes containing the filing cabinets and partition walls which will turn this empty floor into Campaign Headquarters.
For the moment the only person around is VERA KLEIN. *She is in her seventies, and she is bent double with arthritis. She can barely walk, and her head is at ninety degrees to her body. She is sitting at the side by herself, her stick in her hand. She tries to lift her head to speak to us. When she speaks, she has the startling loudness of some deaf people.*

VERA: The most exciting words of my life? 'Common ownership'. To hold things in common, this was our aim. This single phrase produced a thrill in me, like grasping a thin electric wire. Another phrase: 'moral imperative'. This was the language of after the war.
Millions and millions of us. Most of us dead now. Went to war and for the first time met the officer class. The result of meeting them was returning to England and throwing them out.
In those days we thrived on discussion. To disagree meant you were alive. Now it's taken as a sign of disloyalty. What is this fear we have of it now?

SCENE TEN

At once ANDREW *arrives, frantic, bustling across the huge area towards* VERA. *He has papers under his arm and is under considerable stress.*

ANDREW: Oh Vera, I'm sorry, you know we've been looking for you . . .
VERA: Well I've been here.

ANDREW: Yes I know. (*He speaks very loudly into her ear, so she can understand.*) It's our fault. I'm sorry. We've had our problems. Today's the manifesto launch.

VERA: Yes I gathered. Nobody told me.

ANDREW: Didn't they?

VERA: You were lucky I was at home.

ANDREW: Indeed.

(*He looks round a little frantically, trapped with her now.*)

VERA: I didn't know why they'd sent me a taxi. So I thought I'd get in. Nobody told me it was coming.

ANDREW: (*Pretending interest*) Didn't they?

VERA: Still that's the Party nowadays. They send you a car and you do what you're told.

(BRYDEN *comes in, superbly suited and gleaming with life, carrying briefcase and papers.*)

BRYDEN: Vera my dear, I didn't know you'd be with us.

VERA: Nor did I.

ANDREW: We thought it would be nice to put Vera up there for the manifesto launch. As a symbol of roots. And continuity. How Labour goes on. She's on the platform.

BRYDEN: Excellent. (*He turns and shouts at her.*) What a wonderful idea.

VERA: What is?

(BRYDEN *turns and speaks more quietly to* ANDREW.)

BRYDEN: Are you sure there's room for her?

ANDREW: We've got to find her a minder.

(BRYDEN *turns back to* VERA *and addresses her very loudly again.*)

BRYDEN: How are you? How are you keeping?

VERA: Well, I'm in pretty good spirits. I'm not too bad at all.

(*But as she answers,* MALCOLM *has arrived and taken* BRYDEN's *arm. His minder* BRUCE *follows him, keeping up a running commentary on his mobile phone describing* MALCOLM's *every action to an unseen listener.*)

BRUCE: (*Phone*) Malcolm's arriving now at Campaign Headquarters, he's just walking in . . .

MALCOLM: Ah Bryden, thank God you're here.

BRYDEN: Hello Malcolm. (*He nods at* BRUCE.) Bruce.

BRUCE: (*Phone*) He's saying good morning to Bryden.
ANDREW: Good morning, Malcolm.
BRUCE: (*Phone*) Now he's taking Bryden aside to have a short
talk.

(MALCOLM *has led* BRYDEN *away by the arm.*)

MALCOLM: When am I speaking?
BRYDEN: Malcolm you're speaking third.
MALCOLM: Third? Third?
BRUCE: (*Phone*) I don't expect him to be talking for long.
ANDREW: Bryden is opening . . .
BRYDEN: I have to. As Campaign Chairman. Then second
comes the Leader, of course . . .

(VERA *has wandered away, ignored, on her own.* MALCOLM
leans right in to BRYDEN *to make his most urgent point.*)

MALCOLM: Please. It is scripted?
BRYDEN: Malcolm. It's scripted. No worries.
MALCOLM: He's not going into verbal freefall?

(MARY *arrives, absolutely fresh and full of cheer, carrying huge
great charts in her hand.*)

MARY: Good morning all.
ALL: Mary, Mary, good morning.
BRUCE: (*Phone*) He's turning, he's turning, that conversation's
over . . .
MALCOLM: (*To* MARY) You're looking great.
MARY: Well thank you, Malcolm. I've got your grid.
MALCOLM: Oh God. Where are you sending me?
BRUCE: (*Phone*) He's now talking to Mary.
MALCOLM: How many microchip factories? How many
mornings on fruit farms?

(*As* MARY *takes* MALCOLM *aside to talk him through his grid,*
ANDREW *has taken* BRUCE *by the arm.*)

ANDREW: I wonder Bruce, could I have a word?
BRUCE: Yes of course. No problem. (*He speaks into his phone.*)
I'll just put you on hold. I have to go face-to-face.

(*We can hear* MARY'*s conversation drifting across meanwhile.*)

MARY: It's not too bad, I promise, there's an ice-cream
factory . . .

(*Now* OLIVER *comes in and addresses everyone at once.*)

52

OLIVER: Is everyone ready? If everyone's ready, I think we can start.

(He waits for a reaction, but no one takes any notice. ANDREW has led BRUCE to a corner.)

ANDREW: Bruce, I wondered, Vera here needs a minder. I was wondering if you could look after her this morning . . .

BRUCE: No way. No way, Andrew. I can't leave Malcolm. Malcolm's not going anywhere without me.

ANDREW: I can ask Malcolm.

BRUCE: Don't you dare. He's mine. I'm not bloody doing it . . .

ANDREW: Oh for God's sake, look, it won't be for long.

(But BRUCE has already turned away to go back to MALCOLM.)

BRUCE: Malcolm, I'm sorry sir, excuse me, I've got your aftershave . . .

(ANDREW turns in dismay.)

ANDREW: Oh God . . .

(But LINDSAY has already come running on, leaving a bewildered little group of men at the side of the stage.)

LINDSAY: Andrew . . .

ANDREW: Yes?

LINDSAY: There's six doctors waiting . . .

ANDREW: Six?

LINDSAY: Yes, you wanted discontented doctors on the platform to sit beside George . . .

(ANDREW shakes his head.)

ANDREW: Not six!

LINDSAY: They've all got speeches prepared.

ANDREW: Oh my God . . .

(But MALCOLM, having combed his hair and patted his cheeks with aftershave, is now heading back towards ANDREW.)

MALCOLM: Look Andrew, I do have to say to you, I do hope that woman is not going to speak.

ANDREW: Which woman?

MALCOLM: Flaming Vera. If Vera speaks, I am leaving. Because she is right off her head . . .

(LINDSAY has gone out again. ANDREW is nodding. OLIVER is calling across to him to get everything together.)

53

ANDREW: Yes I know . . .

OLIVER: Andrew! Andrew!

    (GWENDA *now comes running on.*)

GWENDA: Andrew what the hell's going on? We were meant to
    get a sound-test . . .

ANDREW: I know . . .

GWENDA: Before the press got here. To try out the music.

    (GWENDA *is close to* VERA *as she says this last word and* VERA
    hears it.)

VERA: Music? I hate music. It buggers my machinery.

GWENDA: (*Very loud*) Then why don't you turn your apparatus off?

    (LINDSAY *has returned with a small group of uniformed*
    NURSES.)

LINDSAY: Andrew, these nurses have come to join us.

ANDREW: Nurses? Uh-huh.

LINDSAY: Yes, but they're prepared to speak very fast.

ANDREW: That's good. That's good.

NURSE: We've all prepared speeches.

LINDSAY: About their intolerable conditions.

    (*They both smile.* BRYDEN *is in animated conversation with*
    MALCOLM. MARY *is tapping away at a computer terminal.*
    BRUCE *is on the mobile phone.* OLIVER *is moving agitatedly*
    back and forth between the Press who are now seen to be
    assembling at the back of the room itself. GWENDA *is turning*
    VERA's *earpiece off.* ANDREW *looks round in exaggerated*
    satisfaction.)

ANDREW: Good, well this all seems to be going quite well.

    (GEORGE *comes in,* TREVOR *just behind him. He is in a*
    beautiful black suit with red tie and his speech in his hand. First
    day of school. There is sudden silence at his appearance.)

ANDREW: Ah George, yes.

GEORGE: Good morning. Good morning everyone. Vera, I didn't
    know you'd be here.

VERA: Well I am.

GEORGE: Good. Good. Great to see you.

    (*There is a silence. No one quite knows what to do next.*)

ANDREW: Can someone . . . I was just wondering. We do need
    someone to look after Vera.

(But before anyone can volunteer, OLIVER *comes urgently back on.)*

OLIVER: For God's sake, Andrew, we have to start now.

*(*GEORGE *turns round smiling.)*

GEORGE: Everyone ready? And know what you'll say? Some brief introductory statements. And then I will outline our major themes.

(Everyone stands nervously. The Press are seen to have assembled at the back and to be waiting.)

ANDREW: All right, line up, line up please everyone. Get ready.

MARY: OK Vera?

VERA: Yes thank you.

MARY: Head forwards.

(The four politicians are now in a line, facing sideways. GEORGE, *then* BRYDEN, *then* MALCOLM, *then* VERA. *They stand a few moments, like two Flanagan and Allens, waiting for their cue. Suddenly* GEORGE *does a check.)*

GEORGE: Tie. Teeth. Wallet.

(Then as OLIVER *reappears to collect them music begins to play.)*

MALCOLM: My God, what is that?

ANDREW: That is the music.

BRYDEN: Blimey Moses. Do we walk out to that?

MALCOLM: It's incredible.

GEORGE: Isn't it?

MALCOLM: Yes. I didn't know Hitler composed.

OLIVER: Are you ready?

(But GWENDA *runs in again at the last moment.)*

GWENDA: Andrew, we've just got some teachers who are willing to speak, they're willing to say the schools are out of control.

ANDREW: Yeah, tell them hold on, we are coming. *(He turns to* GEORGE.) George?

GEORGE: Yes. *(He turns back to the others.)* This is it. Let's do it like last time. Only this time we win.

(At once the music surges in a Wagnerian swell of power and emotion. The three men lead off and as they go all their

55

minders and followers leave in their wake. They disappear into the crowd at the back of the stage which parts to greet them, then as they climb the stage we are confronted with a massive video image of them all raising their joined arms above their heads together in a victory salute.

VERA *is left behind on the empty stage. The music swells.*)

VERA: When? Someone tell me. When do we start?

ACT TWO: FRIENDLY FIRE

SCENE ONE

Outside a television studio. TREVOR AVERY *stands alone on the stage and talks directly to us.*

TREVOR: The Protection Branch is good. It's a good posting.
According of course to who you get. There are certain
Ministers – I'm not going to name them but let's say they like
climbing in and out of tanks wearing flak jackets – they're
the ones who treat you like dirt.
That isn't George. George is popular. When you go the
theatre, he always asks you what you thought of the play. I
always say, 'Very good play, sir.' That means no one tried to
kill him while he was there.
What's thrown is mostly quite harmless. The eggs are easy.
The tomatoes you see from far off. No, the tricky bit is not
when the public turns violent. It's when the politicians
decide to fight back.

SCENE TWO

As soon as he finishes speaking, TREVOR *turns and the lights reveal a
large TV studio. Above the stage hang batteries of arc lights and huge
monitors. In the background, not yet lit, we can make out two chairs
set out in the adversarial format against a set with cameras
surrounding. Nearer us there is a large area in which a buffet table has
been improvised to offer hospitality and which also offers areas with
chairs and tables at which guests can change and be made up.*
    TREVOR *joins* GEORGE *who is just arriving at the studio. As he
comes in and starts to take his coat off, three women approach him
from different directions.* GWENDA *is looking frantic as ever, trying to
find him;* MARY *is sitting waiting for him, surrounded by page upon
page of opened newspapers; and* LINDSAY *is approaching from
another direction carrying something behind her back. Behind them,
throughout the subsequent scene, the studio itself is made ready for an*

impending interview. Everyone is in a wonderful mood.

GWENDA: Ah George, there you are, thank goodness . . .

MARY: I told you. No problem. Of course he is here.

> (*She spreads out her arms to display him to* GWENDA. *They all smile.*)

GEORGE: Of course.

MARY: And on time.

> (GWENDA *at once offers the cup she is holding.*)

GWENDA: I've brought you water.

MARY: (*Offering another cup*) I've brought you soup.

> (LINDSAY *produces something from behind her back.*)

LINDSAY: Orange juice.

GEORGE: Hey, that's marvellous. I'll have some of each.

> (*They all laugh as he moves across towards the make-up area and starts to undress, taking off his jacket.* GWENDA *has a new shirt prepared.*)

MARY: That's great.

LINDAY: How's your voice?

GEORGE: Oh holding up.

> (*He starts doing actor's voice exercises as they all settle in around him in the dressing area.* GWENDA *goes out to busy herself with the preparations.*)

GEORGE: Mee-mee-mah. Mah-mah-mee-mee-mah.

LINDSAY: How was Swindon?

GEORGE: Swindon was fine. And so was Southampton.

MARY: Southampton was great.

GEORGE: So was Bristol.

LINDSAY: Exeter?

MARY: Exeter was good.

> (GWENDA *has reappeared.*)

GWENDA: George, they need you for make-up.

GEORGE: Which one was Exeter?

> (*But before anyone can answer,* ANDREW *has appeared in his overcoat and carrying an overnight bag.*)

GEORGE: Oh my Lord, look, Andrew's here.

ANDREW: I'm back!

> (*He stands a moment, faking exhaustion. They all greet him.*)

LL: Hello Andrew. Andrew! Hello stranger!

MARY: You all right?

ANDREW: Yes. Though I do think I drew the short straw.

LINDSAY: You did.

(*He starts to take his coat off and* GEORGE *smiles across at him as he puts his fresh shirt on.*)

ANDREW: At least you lot have each other's company . . .

(GWENDA *arrives with fresh liquids.*)

GWENDA: Would you like orange juice?

ANDREW: The advance-man is always out on his own.

(*They all smile, familiar with this complaint as* ANDREW *sits down, full of cheerful self-pity.*)

I have to say, I did actually have the ultimate election experience. The all-time story, you know. I woke up this morning in an hotel room. I rang down to reception, I said, I'm sorry, I have a question. Will you please tell me what town am I in?

(*They all laugh.*)

MARY: And where were you?

ANDREW: Kidderminster.

MARY: Really?

(*He seizes an abandoned packet of biscuits.*)

ANDREW: Oh are those Hob-nobs? They look really good.

MARY: You're gaining weight. You all right?

ANDREW: I'm fine. No worries.

(GEORGE *looks across at him a moment, then touches his arm, a sudden tenderness, as if* GEORGE *wants to say thank you.*)

GEORGE: He's the butcher's dog. He's never ill.

(GEORGE *looks up and finds* OLIVER *standing opposite him.* OLIVER *has not taken off his long blue overcoat and is standing with a quiet gravity which contrasts with everyone else's high spirits.*)

OLIVER: These are your cards.

GEORGE: Oh hello Oliver . . . (*He passes* OLIVER *and smiles at him as he goes to sit down in his new shirt in the make-up chair. He smiles at the* MAKE-UP GIRL *as she starts.*) Good evening.

OLIVER: These are the questions which are bound to come up. Kendrick's attack on you yesterday.

GEORGE: Yeah. That's fine. Did you see him?

(*He turns to the others to make sure they hear.*)

GEORGE: Kendrick in the middle of his speech! He looked at his watch. I couldn't believe it. I thought, he's even lost his own attention!

OLIVER: George, we need a full rehearsal. Of each of these questions.

GEORGE: Sure. No problem.

OLIVER: Now?

GEORGE: Yes. In a minute.

(OLIVER *is standing waiting as if very slightly impatient. But* GEORGE *is being made up and looks at him casually.*)

If I have time.

(LINDSAY *has slipped in beside him and is now sitting on the edge of the make-up desk next to* GEORGE *holding a sheaf of faxes.* GEORGE *at once knows what it is. He speaks lightly, masking his nervousness.*)

So, what's the news?

LINDSAY: Well . . .

GEORGE: You'd better tell me.

LINDSAY: It's good. It's good. It isn't bad. No really, it's fine. (*She smiles apologetically.*) It isn't bad. Honestly. I mean, it's complex. It's as you already know it is.

GEORGE: I see. (*He turns ironically to* OLIVER.) Well that's very helpful.

(*But* LINDSAY *remains serious.*)

LINDSAY: George, you know. It's too close to call.

(ANDREW *and* MARY *have now appeared in the same area to listen to this.*)

GEORGE: That's what I've heard.

LINDSAY: The women aren't churning. I don't know why. The old, the semi-skilled, there we're doing much better.

(ANDREW *smiles, making light of it, not wanting* GEORGE's *mood to dip.*)

ANDREW: They're polls, George. They're polls. Like all polls, they're fallible.

LINDSAY: It'll all be clearer in a few days.

(*There are a couple of nervous looks between the group but*

already MARY *has sat down on the table as well in order to make
sure* GEORGE *is diverted from anxiety about the polls*.)

MARY: They certainly won't vote for us if they read the papers.

GEORGE: The papers! Oh God!

(*She has opened one and* ANDREW *moves round with the
sandwich he has now picked up to look over her shoulder*.)

MARY: This one's so desperate they've commissioned a medium.

ANDREW: Is that the spirit-guide?

MARY: Yeah, that's the one. She's been in touch with a hundred
leading historical characters to find out how they're voting
from inside the grave.

(*Everyone smiles, but* OLIVER *moves away restlessly*.)

The big news is: Winston Churchill is going to vote Tory.

ANDREW: The bad news is: so is Sid James.

(*There is mass laughter*.)

MARY: That's right. And Cecil Rhodes. And Noël Coward. And
Oliver Cromwell.

GEORGE: I see. Do we have anyone at all?

MARY: Yes. Josef Stalin.

GEORGE: Oh well, that's a start I suppose.

(LINDSAY *is reading through her faxes in detail.* GWENDA *is, as
ever, working away at papers on her knees.* TREVOR *is standing
some way away. And* GEORGE's *attention has already swung
away again*.)

Lindsay.

(*She looks up, catching the slight tension in his tone*.)

GEORGE: How about me? How are my ratings?

LINDSAY: Your positives are up. But so are your negatives. (*She
moves across to him again, going through the faxes in her hand*.)
Up on 'would handle a crisis really well'. Up on 'in touch
with people like me'. Way down on 'stable'. But that, we
think, is a statistical glitch.

GEORGE: Why?

LINDSAY: We had trouble with the focus group. It sort of spread
out from one man. He thought you were *Grace* Jones, the
singer . . .

(*Everyone smiles again*.)

So some of his answers were a little bit inappropriate. And he may have influenced the rest of the group.

GEORGE: Yeah, so presumably I'm up with six-foot black Amazons . . .

LINDSAY: Yeah, but you're down on 'can't hold a tune . . .'

(GEORGE *smiles up to thank the departing* MAKE-UP GIRL, *as* GWENDA *simultaneously slips a sandwich in his hand which he sits back to eat.*)

GEORGE: Well the road is good.

MARY: The road is really wonderful. We arrive somewhere in the morning – some distant town where we've never been before – we meet one hundred people and we stay for one hour. By nightfall one thousand people are boasting they met George. And five thousand more know someone who did. That's the effect he has. (*Her eyes are gleaming with pleasure at this story. She looks round.*) Well it's true.

(*Everyone is a little embarrassed at the overtness of* MARY's *love for* GEORGE. *One or two people look down.*)

ANDREW: Yes. Yes. I know it is.

(GEORGE *smiles to try and help cover over the moment.*)

GEORGE: People look me in the eye. I must say that is reassuring. They shake my hand and they look me in the eye.

MARY: Yeah.

GEORGE: It's when they don't meet your eye that they're going to betray you.

(*There is a slight pause. Then he looks across at the dark figure of* OLIVER *in the doorway.*)

Oliver, why are you looking down?

(*It's a joke, and everyone gets it. But* GEORGE *gets up out of the make-up chair at once and leads* OLIVER *away.*)

I'm sorry, OK I can tell you need a word with me. Excuse me, everyone. Come over here.

(*He takes* OLIVER's *arm and leads him to a quiet spot where he stands opposite him.*)

What's going on? Oliver, what's bugging you? You'd better tell me.

(*There is a long silence.* OLIVER *looks down, obviously torn about talking to* GEORGE *at all.*)

OLIVER: George, I just don't like the whole bloody thing.

(GEORGE *looks at him, intent now.*)

GEORGE: What do you mean?

OLIVER: Well look it's just . . . you know everyone's so happy, everyone's saying the campaign's going well. No major upsets. No Pearl Harbor, that kind of thing.
(*He is suddenly quiet.*)

OLIVER: But wars aren't going well when nothing is happening.

GEORGE: It's too quiet, you mean?
(OLIVER *nods.*)

OLIVER: There's no defining issue. It's been seven days. In every election there is one crucial engagement. (*He has moved away from* GEORGE *and now he turns back.*) And what spooks me is . . . there's no sign of it yet.
(GEORGE *is looking at him, sharing his gravity now.*)

GEORGE: No, I know.

OLIVER: Also . . .

GEORGE: What?

OLIVER: I don't like this programme. Linus Frank screwed you last time. Frank is a carnivore.
(GEORGE *is quiet, serious now.*)

GEORGE: So?

OLIVER: I smell a set-up, that's what's shitting me. I tried to get a sight of Linus Frank's clipboard. There's a P.A. who often gives us a clue. She says no one on the programme knows anything.

GEORGE: I don't like that.

OLIVER: There's no bloody paperwork, there's no indication of where Frank's heading at all. Also . . .

GEORGE: What?
(OLIVER *stops, this time really hesitant.*)

OLIVER: No. I can't say.
(OLIVER *looks at him a moment, but* MARY *is already heading over urgently to join them.*)
George, look, I'm not saying anything. I'm just saying watch it, that's all.
(OLIVER *has raised his voice in real alarm, but* MARY *is already upon* GEORGE *to warn him on the next thing.*)

MARY: He's coming.

63

OLIVER: Who?

MARY: Linus Frank's coming. He's on the Scarsdale.

(GEORGE *frowns*.)

GEORGE: The Scarsdale? What the hell does that mean?

MARY: It's a diet. Flatter him.

(*But before* GEORGE *can respond,* LINUS FRANK *is heading towards him. He is a short man, floridly dressed, in his early sixties, with a shock of white hair and a clipboard under his arm. His manner is very smooth.*)

LINUS: George, what a pleasure to welcome you back on my little show.

GEORGE: How are you, Linus? (*He takes one step back to admire* LINUS'S *outline*.) Goodness, are you losing weight?

LINUS: Well I am actually, yes, just a little . . . you noticed?

GEORGE: Oh Linus, please, how could I not? (*He turns to the others, who have all gathered to watch this encounter.*) Look, everyone, have you seen Linus?

ALL: Yeah, yeah.

GEORGE: I wouldn't have known it was you.

(LINUS *swells with pleasure, unaware of the satirical looks behind him.*)

LINUS: The funny thing is – you know who helped me?

GEORGE: No.

LINUS: I got a good tip from the Queen.

GEORGE: Really?

LINUS: Yes.

GEORGE: From the Queen, eh?

LINUS: She said to me, 'In my job, the secret is: never eat pudding.'

GEORGE: Never eat pudding? Ah. Good tip. Interesting. (*He turns to his group who are watching with varying degrees of amusement and disbelief.*) Andrew? You should hear this.

LINUS: And it's completely transformed me . . .

(*He pivots a moment, to show his still considerable girth.*)

GEORGE: Well certainly . . . it works for her.

LINUS: Yes.

GEORGE: She's looking good.

LINUS: She is. God bless her. (*He smiles, going back to business.*)

Now you know the format for this sort of thing.

GEORGE: Yes of course. You're doing all three of us.

LINUS: Yes. I did Kendrick last week.

GEORGE: Ah yes. (*He pauses warily.*) I didn't see it.

LINUS: Really? Oh that's a shame . . . (*He smiles confidentially.*) You know, Kendrick is good. At one-to-one interviews. I mean whatever your differences, you would have to say . . . just as a pro . . . I'm an old pro myself . . . this man is pretty terrific.

(GEORGE *is just watching now, keeping careful silence, not rising to the bait.*)

I suspect secretly you think that as well.

GEORGE: Well . . .

LINUS: Don't you?

(*There is a pause.* GEORGE *is ice-cold.*)

GEORGE: No. No I don't actually. I think he's hopeless. He's also dishonest. That's what I don't like.

LINUS: Really? (*He looks genuinely concerned.*) That makes me sad. I'm sorry you say that. Because he was terribly nice about you.

GEORGE: (*Not giving an inch*) Yes, I'm sure. He can afford to be.

LINUS: Oh, do you think it's just that?

(*The two men look at each other,* GEORGE *trying to keep his temper down.*)

GEORGE: What do you think it is?

LINUS: I don't know, George. Really. (*Then he leans in and touches his arm for the kill.*) Isn't it more a difference of style?

(*At once there is a great cry from the back as the* FLOOR MANAGER *calls out and the studio comes to life.*)

F.M.: THIRTY SECONDS AND COUNTING!

LINUS: Now where am I going?

(*All* GEORGE's *office has overheard this conversation and, as* LINUS *is led away to consult with his people on one side of the area, so* GEORGE's *team now crowd round him on the other side. Suddenly they are like two boxers before a fight.*)

ANDREW: Don't rise to it, George, don't let him get to you . . .

MARY: You know full well he's winding you up.

GEORGE: Yes of course.

65

(GEORGE *looks bitterly across the studio at* LINUS *talking smoothly to his* PRODUCERS *and* ASSISTANTS.)

MARY: He's heard the rumours.

GEORGE: I know. (*He turns, getting genuinely ratty.*) I know what he's doing.

MARY: Everyone tells him you've got a very short fuse. He's trying to rattle you.

GEORGE: For God's sake, of course. You think I can't see that?

ANDREW: He'll work on you, remember, you know he'll work on you . . .

GEORGE: Sure. Sure. I know.

(OLIVER *comes in now to join, definitive.*)

OLIVER: George, never show anger. Anger makes you look weak.

ANDREW: It's the first rule.

OLIVER: Be slow.

ANDREW: Don't be hasty.

OLIVER: Whatever happens, don't come in too quick. If you feel your blood rise, that's when he's winning. Remember. You show anger: he wins. He wins, George.

(OLIVER *is now standing directly opposite* GEORGE *with his hands on his shoulders.*)

GEORGE: Yes. Yes I've got that.

F.M.: TEN SECONDS, EVERYONE.

(*The group round* GEORGE *has expanded now to include* P.A.s *and* FLOOR MANAGERS *waiting to lead him to his place.* LINUS *has gone on ahead and can be seen in the distance checking himself in monitors.* GEORGE *has adjusted his clothes and put his head down for the fight.*)

ALL: Good luck, good luck, George.

GEORGE: No worries. I'll see you all later.

(*He is about to move across the studio floor, when* OLIVER *holds out his hand containing the question cards* GEORGE *has forgotten. His voice is cool.*)

OLIVER: George. The cards. We didn't do the cards.

(GEORGE *looks at him a moment and reaches out to take the cards from him. At once the mighty music of the Linus Frank programme comes crashing in at full volume. As* GEORGE *walks*

66

towards the set, the screens hanging above the studio show the words A NATION DECIDES: WITH LINUS FRANK.)

SCENE THREE

The interview. The two men are immediately in front of us, at the centre of the stage, on the little overlit set which echoes the words A NATION DECIDES. *Above them, monitors showing the live broadcast. Around them, cameras and* P.A.*s prowl. And further off, to one side, are* GEORGE'*s team:* TREVOR, LINDSAY, OLIVER, ANDREW, GWENDA *and* MARY *whose body language, in silhouette, reveals their reactions to how the interview is going. We join it some way in,* LINUS FRANK *spelling out his words clearly,* GEORGE *looking relaxed and confident.*

LINUS: There's a question now, Mr Jones, I'd like to raise with
   you . . . to do, if I may, with your policies . . . and the feeling
   perhaps you've now changed policy so often that no one
   quite knows where your Party stands.
   (GEORGE *smiles, not threatened.*)
GEORGE: Yes of course I've heard that. It's true we've, er,
   changed certain things, certain, er, ideas . . . but of course
   that's just being responsive, just being responsible,
   responding to what people say . . .
LINUS: Yes but surely . . .
   (*Again* GEORGE *smiles easily.*)
GEORGE: If I may just finish. We can't win on this. When Tories
   change policies, it's called flexibility and it's said to show
   strength. When we do it, it's vacillation and people say that
   we're weak.
   (LINUS *is not looking at* GEORGE'*s answer, but already
   consulting his clipboard for the next question which he brings in
   straight away.*)
LINUS: But it does seem, Mr Jones, that on handling the economy
   you still command no real confidence.
GEORGE: I'm not sure that's true.
LINUS: I don't mean your party. No. You see, Mr Jones, let's be

clear, when people say that, they really mean you.

(GEORGE *pauses for just an instant, then they start talking together and overlapping.*)

GEORGE: I'm not sure . . .

LINUS: If I can put to you polls . . .

GEORGE: If you could just . . .

LINUS: No, I'm sorry. I must make this point. People believe you have an uncertain grasp of policy basics.

(GEORGE *smiles, confident after this messy passage.*)

GEORGE: I think I can say that is truly absurd.

LINUS: But is it? Worse for you, some of your own colleagues do doubt you. We've all heard reports of some quite stormy scenes.

(*There is an odd pause.* LINUS *is waiting as if he has asked a question.*)

GEORGE: I'm sorry. I don't know what you're asking.

LINUS: Do you recognize their accusation, which is you're not up to the job?

(*At the side the silhouetted group have moved a little closer, watching nervously.*)

GEORGE: No I don't. Not at all. I've never heard my colleagues say any such thing.

LINUS: An impression of laziness, tetchiness . . .

GEORGE: Yes. This is something the Press likes to create.

(LINUS *sits back, for the first time sensing blood and becoming expansive. Once again they are on top of each other.*)

LINUS: Ah yes, the Press of course . . .

GEORGE: I mean . . .

LINUS: Ah yes. Ah yes. A theme of yours. We hear a lot from you on the Press. I wonder . . .

GEORGE: If I . . .

LINUS: No I think, if I can make one point, maybe it's this obsession with the Press . . .

GEORGE: I only mentioned it once.

LINUS: This extraordinary obsession gives the impression you're somewhat thin-skinned.

(GEORGE *plays this down, knowing he must not rise to it.*)

GEORGE: Not at all. Not at all.

LINUS: You see, it is a fair question, it's not me, it's not me that's raising this . . .

GEORGE: I accept that.

LINUS: I am simply here to voice a popular concern. People do want to know whether someone so prickly . . . so jumpy . . . without any formal education . . .

(GEORGE *smiles at this easy one.*)

GEORGE: Mr Frank, I did go to school.

(*But* LINUS *doesn't let go and they overlap again, not losing their cool, but both trying to use volume to disguise their incoherence.*)

LINUS: No, this is a legitimate anxiety, I won't let you . . .

GEORGE: It's this kind of *snobbery* . . .

LINUS: No formal background . . . I'm saying with little formal grasp . . . you must see this contributes to the popular opinion that Labour is fighting with the wrong man.

(GEORGE *smiles, sitting back on this.*)

GEORGE: That's not true.

LINUS: I mean your own Shadow Chancellor, opinion polls show that if Mr Pryce were Leader of the Party you would be coasting to an eighty-seat win.

(GEORGE *smiles, trying to steady it.*)

GEORGE: If I may . . . I came to talk about policies . . . exciting policies we have . . . real issues . . .

LINUS: But leadership . . . is that not an issue as well? Time and again it is said you are Labour's millstone.

GEORGE: What can I say? All Labour leaders are subject to attack.

LINUS: Is this true? Historically, Hugh Gaitskell, for a start . . .

(GEORGE *comes straight in, not able to resist.*)

GEORGE: Hugh Gaitskell did what Fleet Street required of him. He died very young.

(*He snaps out this last line. The team at the side move at once uneasily.* GEORGE *knows he has just sounded intemperate and* LINUS *is on top of him at once.*)

LINUS: Well that if I . . .

GEORGE: Now I think we're wandering . . . to get back to policy . . . . . .

LINUS: Fleet Street again, Mr Jones. This is a legitimate
question. (*He pauses a second.*) Can Britain be ruled by a
man with a grudge?
(*For the first time* GEORGE *is seriously rattled, but* LINUS
blocks him off.)

GEORGE: Now look . . .

LINUS: Very well, let's change the subject entirely. As you say,
the policies themselves. And how they change. Let's look at
mortgage tax relief.

GEORGE: Ah yes. (*He stops, taken aback by this sudden change of
tack but trying to hide it.*) Yes of course.

LINUS: There is no mention in your manifesto of any plan to
abolish this concession.

GEORGE: No. No we have none.

LINUS: And yet my understanding is, until very recently you
were determined to abolish it.
(GEORGE *looks at him, a flicker of horror appearing on his
face.*)

GEORGE: Abolish it? No, that is absolutely not true.
(LINUS *leans forward, not yielding and* GEORGE *starts
pretending to try to remember.*)

LINUS: You see I've been told, on very good authority, plans to
abolish it were there. They were in the draft manifesto.
Then at the last minute they were removed.
(GEORGE *frowns.*)

GEORGE: I don't think so.

LINUS: On November 14th, on your instructions, a whole
paragraph was specifically removed . . .
(GEORGE *shakes his head.*)

GEORGE: No, I don't think you'll find that is so.

LINUS: You mean you're denying it? You're denying this
proposition was removed?
(GEORGE *leans forward.*)

GEORGE: On mortgage tax relief, it was never my intention . . .
you ask me, I tell you, I want to be clear . . .

LINUS: The truth now, Mr Jones . . .

GEORGE: This proposal was never to appear in the final
manifesto.

LINUS: Ah good yes, now, *now* we're making some headway, so now you admit it was there for a time.

GEORGE: Well . . .

LINUS: So who took it out? That is my question. Did you or did you not take it out?

GEORGE: I did not.

LINUS: Really? *Really?* That's not what I've been told.

(*There is just a moment's pause. LINUS is looking at GEORGE as if defying him to crack. And after a moment GEORGE loses his nerve.*)

GEORGE: Are you calling me a liar?

(*There is a terrible silence. LINUS waits, then smiles very slightly.*)

LINUS: I'm calling you nothing. That is for the public to decide. Thank you, Mr Jones.

(*And he turns at once to end the programme. But as he does GEORGE gets up out of his chair and comes glowering down from the set.*)

SCENE FOUR

At once GEORGE comes raging back into the waiting area where his group have scattered in despair. ANDREW is there to receive him. In the background LINUS FRANK is still in his chair, winding up as the closing music plays him out. As GEORGE storms down from the set, ANDREW cuts him off.

GEORGE: Walk me away, just walk me away from him . . .

ANDREW: All right, George.

GEORGE: What the hell's going on?

(*He stands towering with rage, ANDREW looking round nervously.*)

How did he know? Somebody told him. You tell me, who told him? Who bloody told him?

(*GWENDA has appeared beside GEORGE in order to convey a message. ANDREW gestures to her.*)

ANDREW: Wait, wait a moment . . .

GEORGE: Whoever told him is going to have to face me.
  (*He moves away, shaking with rage.* GWENDA *and* TREVOR *wait nervously.*)
GWENDA: George, Mr Frank would like to say goodnight to you . . .
  (*At once* GEORGE *makes a physical move which suggests he would beat* FRANK *up and* ANDREW *has to block his path.* TREVOR *instinctively moves closer to* GEORGE.)
ANDREW: George, no, George, you're not making this worse . . .
  (MARY *appears, shaking her head, more in sorrow than in anger, as if it were some personal betrayal.*)
MARY: George, oh George, I don't believe it . . .
  (*From the other side* LINDSAY *comes in urgently, as* GWENDA *heads off to convey the message to* LINUS FRANK.)
LINDSAY: It's already started, the phones are ringing out there . . .
MARY: How could you?
GEORGE: He rattled me!
MARY: How *could* you do that?
  (*At once* ANDREW *tries to intervene to prevent things getting worse.*)
ANDREW: Now hold on . . .
MARY: You've handed them everything . . .
GEORGE: I know.
MARY: You've handed them their issue. LABOUR'S SECRET PLAN TO RAISE TAX. You've handed them their headlines . . .
GEORGE: I know that.
  (MARY *turns in despair.*)
MARY: ARE YOU CALLING ME A LIAR? They're all going to use it. Every one! They're going to go for you.
  (*From the side* OLIVER *has appeared, still in his dark coat and completely still, ice-cold with rage and terrifying.*)
OLIVER: He sets the trap and you walk right in.
  (GEORGE *turns.* ANDREW *throws a glance nervously to where* LINUS FRANK *is laughing cheerfully with his* PRODUCER *on the other side of the studio.*)
GEORGE: Oliver . . .

72

(ANDREW *looks nervously between the two men.*)

ANDREW: Now everyone hold on, let's stop for a moment . . .

(OLIVER *is shaking, his voice low.*)

OLIVER: I gave you the cards, it was on the cards I bloody gave you, be careful, it said, watch for it, watch for mortgage tax relief . . .

GEORGE: All right . . .

OLIVER: But oh no! You're too vain to do your bloody homework . . .

(*Again* ANDREW *tries nervously to intervene.*)

ANDREW: Oliver . . .

OLIVER: Of course you're standing round wasting time with these bloody girls.

(GWENDA *has returned and is standing beside* MARY *and* LINDAY, *as* OLIVER's *hand shoots out to point at all three of them.*)

You, you're listening to goo-eyed bloody Mary, all these women surrounding you telling you how marvellous you are . . .

(*Everyone watches appalled as* OLIVER *moves in on* GEORGE.)

Do you not get it? Will you never get it? Giggling with girls who are in love with you. That isn't the job. That's not the bloody job, you idiot.

(*There is a pause in disbelief at what* OLIVER *has just said. Then suddenly* GEORGE *loses control and lunges at* OLIVER *with his fist. He only makes the slightest contact, and at once as the two men fall against each other,* ANDREW *and* TREVOR *are in there to pull* GEORGE *off.*)

ANDREW: Come on, George, come on, get off him! Get off him!

(*They pull the men apart.* MARY *is standing appalled at the side with* GWENDA.)

MARY: This is ridiculous!

LINDSAY: Come on, we're all going nuts . . .

(ANDREW *has looked round frantically and is now bundling the whole group out of the open area where the fight has taken place and is making them walk in a disorderly way back towards the make-up area and buffet.*)

ANDREW: Walk away, quick, let's move, keep moving. Come on,

keep walking . . . keep walking!

LINDSAY: Did anyone see?

(*They stop. They look round.* LINUS *has glanced over, but is still laughing and joking with his* PRODUCER.)

ANDREW: This is suicide.

TREVOR: Come on, gentlemen, let's calm this thing down.

(ANDREW *looks round. There is a sudden silence. People stand round dazed at the suddenness and violence of the outburst, as if not able to believe what has just happened. In the silence* LINDSAY *goes back outside the area and looks out to make sure there is no one about. In the far distance* LINUS *waves goodnight to his team, and tells them he is off to his club. There is the odd scattered sound of people saying goodnight to one another. Some lights go out. Meanwhile* GWENDA *has helped* GEORGE *to sit down.* MARY *has got out a handkerchief to put against* OLIVER's *lip which is bleeding slightly. Then* OLIVER *shakes his head. He sounds shaken.*)

OLIVER: I wanted to talk to you, remember? That's what's so stupid.

(GEORGE *looks round, wary.*)

GEORGE: So?

OLIVER: Before the interview started. I took you aside. Then I thought, no, it's not fair. And you'd made a rule. You gave us a warning.

GEORGE: I did?

(*He is very quiet, as if fearing what will come next.*)

GEORGE: What warning?

OLIVER: Never speak ill of Malcolm Pryce.

(GWENDA *has been to the buffet and got* GEORGE *a glass of water. He takes it from her, unseeing. Then she goes out again.*)

GEORGE: Malcolm?

OLIVER: Sure. Linus had lunch with him.

GEORGE: *Malcolm?*

OLIVER: I wanted to tell you. At the time, I didn't know what it meant. But it just made me nervous.

(GEORGE *looks away. There is a smear of blood on* OLIVER's *lip.*)

OLIVER: I knew that something was wrong.

(*Again, no one speaks as everyone tries to work this out.* MARY *looks round.*)

MARY: I don't understand. You're not saying Malcolm would do this deliberately?

GEORGE: It's out of the question.

OLIVER: No. George is right. (*He smiles bitterly.*) I'd guess Malcolm was boasting. Because it was his scheme in the first place. It was his baby. He dreamt it up. (*He shakes his head.*) I can just hear him. Good food and good claret. Sitting there gossiping in the Garrick, in the big leather chairs . . . 'I had this great scheme. Then guess what? George overruled it . . .'

ANDREW: Yes. Oh yes. It begins to make sense . . .

(ANDREW *is nodding.* GEORGE *has turned away, knowing this is the truth.*)

OLIVER: I'm sure he wasn't out to betray us. Not deliberately. Malcolm's far too disloyal to be openly disloyal. But he does have a weakness. And it's one which is common among Labour politicians . . . (*Suddenly he releases all his contempt.*) He'll say anything if you give him posh lunch.

(ANDREW *gets up, suddenly furious.*)

ANDREW: They just don't see it!

OLIVER: I know . . .

ANDREW: They just never get it! (*He turns, indignant.*) God, don't you hate socialists? You give them one drink or one meal. Then they open the door because they just can't resist it. And all at once the shit's pouring through.

(GWENDA *has reappeared in the half-light. She stands nervously, not wanting to interrupt.*)

GWENDA: George, I'm sorry. The car is outside for you. I think perhaps . . . we've parked it round the back. I'm afraid the Press is out there at the front.

MARY: OK.

GWENDA: They're all asking if there's going to be a statement.

(GEORGE *gets up.*)

GEORGE: No. We're saying nothing tonight. (*Before anyone can speak he raises a hand.*) We can survive this. But only if I get Malcolm on side. That's the priority. Mary, I have to see Malcolm myself.

(MARY *is about to speak, but again* GEORGE *interrupts before she can.*)

Yes, if necessary we both stop campaigning. The issue is me. I'm now the issue. And Malcolm's the only man who can help.

(*He turns to go. It is dark now in the studio, and they look like a little bunch of conspirators. But after a few steps* GEORGE *turns back.*)

What happened in here . . . I mean between us . . . (*He nods at* OLIVER.) It didn't happen, all right? Not even in your memoirs?

OLIVER: Yes. Yes, of course, George.

ANDREW: Yes.

MARY: Yes.

LINDSAY: No problem.

(*They have all spoken at once. Now there is an awkward moment, as if* GEORGE *wanted to speak to* OLIVER *and apologize. But he doesn't. He just nods.*)

GEORGE: Thank you. Good. Let's get back to work.

(GEORGE *goes out, followed by* TREVOR. *The group stand saddened, heads bowed, frozen for a moment, no one daring to speak. Then* OLIVER *turns and silently goes out the other way.*)

SCENE FIVE

The group scatters and GWENDA *appears at the side to speak to us. At first her tone is quiet.*

GWENDA: You see, they are different. Politicians are different. The good ones surprise you again and again. George's reaction to what had just happened was to behave as if nothing had happened at all.

(*Behind her, the music of the Labour theme tune has begun to play. Now it swells, and on to the stage comes* GEORGE *on the stump, seen both in person and on the huge video screens above the stage. He is pushing his way through crowds of people,*

76

*shaking hands with everyone in his path, and greeting people one
by one.* MARY *is at his side, as he pushes on relentlessly through.
He calls out to tell* REPORTERS *how confident he's feeling:* 'I'm
feeling great, I'm feeling wonderful,' *he says and puts both
thumbs up in a gesture of implacable gaiety. Then he begins to
back away, laughing and smiling.* 'We're going to win this one,
no question, we're going to win it. I mean it. We're really going to
win it.' *The lights start to fade and the crowd scatters around him
as he gives his last smiles, backing away all the time.*)
And then one day we stopped. As it happened at an aircraft
factory.
(*The stage is suddenly deserted, the crowd gone, the music dies.
There is a moment's silence.*)
We stopped and finally we found him some time.

SCENE SIX

An aircraft hangar. GEORGE *is standing on one side with* MARY *and*
GWENDA *beside him. They wait a few moments. Then* MALCOLM
PRYCE, *obviously summoned, arrives briskly with* BRUCE. *As soon as
the men are together, the three minders all turn and silently leave, as on
cue. The two men look at each other across the great space.*

GEORGE: Ah Malcolm . . .
MALCOLM: Yes.
    (*He waits a moment.* GEORGE *is quite still.*)
    I got a message. I'm meant to be in Edinburgh.
GEORGE: Yes. Yes I know. (*He looks at him a moment.*) I'm meant
    to be in Burnley. But I've postponed it.
MALCOLM: The result is I'm in a bloody bad mood.
GEORGE: Uh-huh.
    (MALCOLM *has intended this as a nervous joke. But* GEORGE *is
    still not moving towards him.*)
MALCOLM: Well . . . we're doing pretty well.
GEORGE: Yes. Yes it seems so.
MALCOLM: The surprising thing is, the polls have held up.
GEORGE: Surprising?

MALCOLM: I mean . . . after your trouble in the papers.

GEORGE: Ah yes . . .

>   (MALCOLM *smiles nervously.*)

MALCOLM: GEORGE IN BLUNDERLAND. But it seems
>   we've survived.

>   (GEORGE *doesn't answer, just lets him hang.*)

>   I want to be clear . . . I know there've been rumours . . . for
>   instance, there are people in your office . . . and they are
>   trying to stick the whole thing on me. I did lunch with
>   Frank. It's true. But we stuck to deep background. The
>   timing was just an unfortunate coincidence.

GEORGE: Good. Thank you. (*He smiles.*) Meanwhile I was
>   hoping we might have a talk.

>   (MALCOLM *looks at him warily.* GEORGE *is apparently
>   guileless, but* MALCOLM *is on his guard.*)

MALCOLM: A talk?

GEORGE: Of course. You must see. I'm not in an easy position.
>   The last two days have been pretty tough . . .

MALCOLM: I know.

GEORGE: So now I'm thinking, OK, *now* we need to retrieve
>   this. (*He turns and smiles at* MALCOLM.) This is the moment
>   I turn to my friends.

>   (MALCOLM *looks even more deeply distrustful of* GEORGE's
>   *drift and apparent openness.*)

MALCOLM: Ah, I see.

GEORGE: Well yes. I mean in the past . . . you and I, Malcolm
>   . . . we've joked about it. We've laughed at the Tories. Our
>   jealousy of how they seem to do these things right. In
>   private they all know Kendrick's a fool. Yet the great thing
>   is: they never say so. For them it's the great political
>   imperative. (*He pauses a second.*) You must always talk the
>   Leadership up.

>   (MALCOLM *frowns, earnest.*)

MALCOLM: We have tried, George . . .

GEORGE: Have you?

MALCOLM: Certainly. We have been trying. In every interview I
>   mention your name. I always say: 'This man is our Leader.'
>   (*He says it firmly, but* GEORGE *just looks at him.*)

GEORGE: Yes. I'm sure you do. But that's hardly effusive. Don't you also have to say I lead you quite well?
(MALCOLM *holds his ground.*)
MALCOLM: I think I do, George. I think I imply that. I think it's clear. I don't think you can lay these things on too thick.
GEORGE: Don't you? I do. (*A sudden, unmistakable steel has entered his voice.*) You see we've reached the stage where thick's how I want it. From now on, Malcolm, I want it as thick as you can.
(MALCOLM *shifts once more, uneasy.*)
MALCOLM: Now come on, George, please, we do have to be sensible.
GEORGE: Do we?
MALCOLM: There is an intelligent electorate out there. If I suddenly start screaming George Jones is a genius, do you think they won't know there's something odd going on?
(*Now* GEORGE *frowns, not at all put out by the implied insult.*)
GEORGE: Odd? Why? Because you so obviously don't actually believe it . . .
MALCOLM: Oh come on now, George . . .
GEORGE: Because it would be such an obvious break from what you've been saying so far . . .
MALCOLM: You know that's not true.
GEORGE: Isn't it? (*He looks at* MALCOLM, *unmistakably tough now.*) No, I think what's more conspicuous is when, as recently, you say nothing at all.
(MALCOLM *looks at him, beginning to get tougher himself and to go on to the attack.*)
MALCOLM: George, I don't quite know what you're implying. This is something we're all rather tired of, you know.
GEORGE: Oh really?
MALCOLM: Yes. Whenever you're in trouble, whenever you yourself have messed something up, then you don't stop and think, you don't *examine* what's happened, oh no, the first thing you do is look round for a scapegoat. (*He pauses, lethally.*) Then you send out the bully-boys and duff someone up.
(GEORGE *looks at him impassively.*)

GEORGE: The bully-boys?

MALCOLM: Yes. (*He looks at* GEORGE, *unforgiving.*) You know who I mean by that.

GEORGE: My private office, is that who you mean?

MALCOLM: George's sycophants.

GEORGE: Oh really? Is that what they're called?

(GEORGE *smiles slightly, but* MALCOLM *is carrying on, not humoured.*)

MALCOLM: Yes they are. And worse. You don't know the half of it. George, you live in a world of your own. It's a world your own little team has created. And in which you never hear that anything's wrong.

GEORGE: Oh is that right?

MALCOLM: Yes it is. I've seen them do it to you. They whip the newspapers away before you can read them. They turn off the telly so you don't see the news . . . (*He has moved now, a genuine indignation in his voice.*) Oh come on for God's sake, George, everyone's saying it. Even you must see it. You're embalmed in flattery. You've let yourself become the prisoner of a group . . .

GEORGE: That's absurd!

MALCOLM: And this group have rotted you. No one can get near you. No one can even get to talk to you unless they have permission from Oliver Dix.

(GEORGE *is immediately defensive.*)

GEORGE: That's fair. That's his job. He's my lieutenant.

MALCOLM: I know. You have a lieutenant with a black belt in karate. And given to spouting long passages from Sun Tzu's *The Art of War.*

GEORGE: So what?

MALCOLM: Another way of putting it: a swivel-eyed lunatic, whose actual function is clear. To reassure his leader, come hell or high water, that nothing is ever his fault.

GEORGE: That's simply not true.

(GEORGE *is offended, but* MALCOLM *has begun to enjoy himself.*)

MALCOLM: I saw him once, George, I promise you, I met Oliver at the airport with his family. I'd always thought this man is a little bit strange. He was going on holiday. Under his arm he had an American business book on transactional analysis, and two biographies of Hitler. (*He shakes his head.*) What the hell has that got to do with socialism?

GEORGE: All right, he's eccentric.

MALCOLM: George, I'm only telling you what everyone says. (*He turns again on* GEORGE *in full flow.*) Do you think people don't realize? Do you think they're not hurt by this? Seeing you in the tea-room with the same unelected clique every day? Goodness, my God, you come to me now and ask for my loyalty. You ask me to talk your Leadership up. But if you'd spent the time with us, with your own Shadow Cabinet, that you spent with your dear friends Andrew and Oliver, then perhaps that loyalty would already be there.

GEORGE: I see. (*He is looking at him coldly, the anger making him low and dangerous.*) I see. Have you thought . . . I mean I'm just asking this . . . has it occurred to you why I created that office? Why I had to bring these good people in? (*He waits a moment.*) I did it because I needed some colleagues I could actually rely on . . .

MALCOLM: You could rely on us!

GEORGE: . . . and who I could guarantee would do what I say. (MALCOLM *turns away in disgust, but* GEORGE *just shakes his head.*)

You wait, you just wait, I can't wait to see it. You try leading the Party, you try sitting in that room every day, listening to this procession of whingeing comrades, who all troop in to tell you what you're doing wrong . . . (*He turns, full of contempt.*) There was, I swear to you, no problem too trivial, there wasn't a twinge of conscience too fine, that people didn't feel 'oh I know . . . I know what to do now, I think I'll go in and explain this to George . . .' (*He moves away, bitter.*) I mean it's hard not to laugh, you start to laugh openly at these ridiculous self-important MPs, who all think their own special reasons, their own special *reasoning*, their own bloody *consciences* are so much more important than delivering their vote . . . (*He nods.*) So yes, I admit, yes, after two years of it, after two years as the nation's most elevated agony aunt, yes,

I did say: I need a filter. I just need an instrument.
(*He looks steadily at* MALCOLM.) I have to have this if I'm not
to go mad.

(MALCOLM *looks at him, serious now.*)

MALCOLM: Yes, well you have it. You have your instrument. It
does what you want it to. It bullies. It instructs. (*He is
suddenly quiet.*) But now I'm afraid, you need people's real
loyalty. And suddenly you find you've left it too late.
(*But* GEORGE *is shaking his head.*)

GEORGE: It wasn't the office. My office didn't change things.

MALCOLM: What, you think there was resentment from the start?

GEORGE: Yes, of course.

MALCOLM: Why?

GEORGE: Partly just snobbery.

MALCOLM: Snobbery?

GEORGE: Of course. The People's Party, you know. Never
underestimate its capacity for sheer condescension. They
don't like a Leader without a degree.

MALCOLM: Oh really, George . . .

GEORGE: You don't believe it? One of my own backbenchers said
to me, 'this absurd love of the theatre you fake'. Fake? *Fake?*
'Of course,' he said. 'You can't hope to understand
Shakespeare when you don't have the tools . . .'
(MALCOLM *is shaking his head.*)

MALCOLM: And you think that was it? That was the reason?

GEORGE: No. Of course not.

MALCOLM: Then what?
(GEORGE *raises his voice as if it were obvious.*)

GEORGE: Because of the project! Because of the analysis! (*He is
suddenly exasperated.*) For God's sake, because I brought the
Party bad news!

MALCOLM: You believe it was that?

GEORGE: I'm sure it was. I shut down the fantasy factory. I told
this Party it had to grow up. I made it contemplate reality. I
told it to get serious or else it would remain unelectable. (*He
suddenly smiles.*) Do you think the MPs didn't hate me for
that?
(MALCOLM *just watches, not answering.*)

Of course they did. I used to watch them. They were like naughty schoolboys. They knew in their hearts, they *knew* what had to be done. But they were going to make the person who brought the change suffer. (*He smiles.*) They were never going to give me credit for telling the truth.

(MALCOLM *smiles, a deadly humour in him now.*)

MALCOLM: I see. Well I must say that's a convenient version . . .

GEORGE: It's not a *version*.

MALCOLM: I've never seen things in that particular light. (*He frowns.*) Let me get this clear. Your problem with the Party was, they couldn't stand the fact you got everything right!

GEORGE: In a way. Yes.

(GEORGE *looks at him unapologetic. But* MALCOLM *has become suddenly dry and incisive.*)

MALCOLM: I must say, I think, George, this is not my recollection. In my recollection there was another factor at work.

GEORGE: What was that?

(*There is a silence. Suddenly* MALCOLM *tenses, not answering.*) Please. Go ahead. Say. (*He is level, quiet, as if he knows what is coming.*) We've spent years not having this talk.

MALCOLM: Very well. (*He pauses a moment, knowing he will cross a bridge. Then quietly.*) Everyone respects you. Everyone likes you. No one will ever deny you've got guts. But finally, people don't follow you. Because they know you can't cut it.

(*There is a pause.* GEORGE *takes a couple of steps away, then answers quietly.*)

GEORGE: Well thank you, Malcolm. That's very clear.

(MALCOLM *is unemotional now, the case laid out with clarity.*)

MALCOLM: I look back, George, I tell you I can't count the occasions. Times beyond number. Charles Kendrick is not a brilliant man. We've walked in the Chamber. The whole Parliamentary Party has lined up on some issue, waiting for you to move in and deliver the one hammer blow that would rock this government back. And instead, we've watched you get up, launch in and then fumble. (*He spreads his arms out.*) Oratorical free fall! The Oxford English Dictionary on speed! Every bloody time you funk it. (*He looks down.*) Well, isn't that nearer the truth of this thing?

(GEORGE *is already shaking his head, enraged by the familiarity of the charge.*)

GEORGE: That's the myth, of course. It's been carefully nurtured. Every day, in the papers, they go back to it. Day after day. All right, that's what you expect. What I don't expect is to hear it repeated by my own Shadow Chancellor.

MALCOLM: I've been there! For God's sake, I've seen you!

(GEORGE *shakes his head, suddenly paranoid, emphatic.*)

GEORGE: You try it. You try entering the Chamber. You have two hundred people at your back. And it's you who forced them to abandon what they like to believe are their dearest-held principles. So all they're hoping is you're going to fall flat on your face . . . (*He turns, his bitterness frightening now.*) Like all Labour Leaders, I don't quake before the enemy. It's friendly fire that destroys you. We all go down to the shots from behind. (*He stands, melancholy.*) Because this Party never learns. Not really. Finally, it's only interested in its own sense of what's right. It gives its love only to its dreamers. It never cares if they're effective or not.

(*He smiles. He looks round at* MALCOLM, *who is stilled by* GEORGE's *quiet sincerity.*)

It happened the first day that I got into Parliament. I was introduced to one of those fine old heroes of the Left. White hair. Waistcoat. They said to me, oh he's such a fine man. He speaks so well. He's so wise. His life is spent doing good. But as I listened I thought . . . this is too easy. Doing good is easy. The world needs people who'll fight evil as well. (*He nods, speaking from the heart.*) Yes, and that's a much dirtier business, much harder, it needs much more discipline, it needs much more skill . . . (*He turns and looks at* MALCOLM.) I tell you what, Malcolm, it means being serious.

MALCOLM: And you think that I'm not?

(GEORGE *smiles.*)

GEORGE: I don't know, Malcolm. You're like a lot of people in the Labour Party. You want to be its Leader one day. A life in Labour Party politics. The gossip. The factions. The

84

arguments . . . (*He shakes his head.*) And I fear for you
that's enough.

MALCOLM: That isn't true!

GEORGE: Oh isn't it? Then why are you not really fighting? Why
is there only one man in the whole Shadow Cabinet who's
going round the country doing what I really need? There's
one man among you who never fails to talk my Leadership
up.

(MALCOLM *looks down, knowing* GEORGE *is right.*)
Yes. Bryden Thomas. And why does he do it? Because it's
what good soldiers do. (*He nods.*) That's right. He belongs
to a certain generation. He's older than you are. He
understands. You give it everything. You do your duty.

(MALCOLM *looks at him, suddenly enraged.*)

MALCOLM: What? And you're telling me that I don't?

(GEORGE *just looks at him, not yielding. Then* MALCOLM
*begins to speak very quietly, reaching the really damaging things
he has to say.*)
All right, George, I'll tell you. The fact is, I like you. I've
always liked you. You're a very decent man. But for some
time now the truth is, we've carried you.

(GEORGE *flickers slightly.*)
Yes. And I think you know that as well. (*He looks down.*)
Perhaps you've realized, before this election, a group of us
. . . well it will hardly surprise you. We did get together.
We met to decide. We could have moved in. But we didn't.
For reasons which you may not understand.

(*There is a moment.* GEORGE *looks away, genuinely stunned.*)

MALCOLM: Yes. This Party, of which today you seem to be so
contemptuous . . . the people you think are self-obsessed
and absurd . . . these very people still love you, even while
they despair of you. They said George deserves this . . .

(GEORGE *looks away, lost now.*)
He deserves one more shot at this thing.

(GEORGE *looks at him guiltily, not knowing how to react.*)
If you ask me why, I would say our reasons were
honourable. The Tories get rid of their Leaders when it's
clear they might not win. But we hold on to ours. (*He*

85

pauses.) I call that decency.

(GEORGE *turns to look at him. But* MALCOLM *shakes his head slightly.*)

Perhaps you feel it's pleasure in watching them lose.

(*There is a moment and then* GEORGE *moves in order to reconcile himself with* MALCOLM. *But* MALCOLM *now snaps out of his tone of more-in-sorrow-than-in-anger, and decisively winds up the meeting.*)

GEORGE: Malcolm . . .

MALCOLM: All right, thank you, George. I'll do what you ask of me. I'll go round the country and tell everyone that you're a very fine man. If that's what you want, then that's what I'll do for you.

(GEORGE *looks at him, shaken.*)

GEORGE: It's not for me. It's what has to be done.

(MALCOLM *nods slightly. Then he stops and looks hard at* GEORGE.)

MALCOLM: It isn't the Party. It's not that the Party don't believe in you, you know. (*He moves across and puts his hand on* GEORGE's *arm.*) I say this in love. They smell that you don't believe in yourself.

(*He turns and goes out.* GEORGE *is left alone in the empty aircraft hangar. He looks away a moment. Then he turns and goes out.*)

SCENE SEVEN

Immediately into the Election Party Headquarters come ANDREW, *who has fistfuls of paper in his hands, pursued quickly by* MARY *who is carrying a long coil of fax. Most of the deserted headquarters are darkened, and the light is centred round the desk at which* ANDREW *has been working. The long empty corridors cast huge shadows in the night.*

MARY: Andrew . . .

ANDREW: What?

MARY: Oh Andrew . . .

(*He has sat down at the desk. He takes one look at her as she heads across towards him.*)

ANDREW: Don't tell me.

MARY: I'm afraid so. Look, there's another lot . . .

ANDREW: All right. Let me see. (*He takes the faxes from her and looks at them. Then he gets up, looking at her in despair.*) What's happening? You tell me what's happening. It's all so sudden. That's what I don't get.

(*MARY is walking round the room distractedly in near-panic. ANDREW has moved away from the desk and is shaking his head.*)

We were going great. I thought we were surviving. I even thought we'd limited the Linus Frank thing.

MARY: This is just wham! From nowhere!

(*ANDREW stands as if the answer were somewhere in the darkness.*)

ANDREW: Mary, what are they thinking? Why are they slipping away?

(*BRYDEN has appeared. He is wearing a thick overcoat against the winter cold, and carrying a briefcase. His manner is grave.*)

Bryden. Hey!

BRYDEN: Good evening.

ANDREW: I wasn't expecting you. I thought you were out on the road. You know that I'm meeting George . . .

BRYDEN: Yes, I heard.

ANDREW: He's just popping in on his way home. I've got the first draft of his big speech for Monday. He wanted to work on it over the weekend.

BRYDEN: Good.

(*He has put his things down and is taking his coat and scarf off at one of the tables.* ANDREW *frowns slightly.*)

ANDREW: What about you? Are you going to see him?

BRYDEN: I hope so. I got a call.

ANDREW: From him?

BRYDEN: No. From Lindsay. To come in this evening.

(ANDREW *looks round, confused.*)

ANDREW: From Lindsay?

BRYDEN: Yes. (*He looks at* ANDREW, *checking his surprise.*) Yes.

As it happens. And what she was saying made a good deal of sense.

(*At the back* LINDSAY *has appeared. She is also wrapped against the cold and she has the same serious manner as* BRYDEN. *She stops, seeing* ANDREW. *The darkness and shadow around her make the meeting look conspiratorial.*)

LINDSAY: Good evening.

ANDREW: Lindsay. (*He looks round.*) Lindsay, what's going on here?

MARY: I'm sorry, Andrew. I thought you knew.

ANDREW: No. Am I the only one out of this? Will somebody tell me why everyone's here?

(*He smiles, half-angry, half-amused.* LINDSAY *has taken her coat off and is standing at the table's edge.*)

LINDSAY: I wanted a meeting. I wanted an emergency session. We got hold of George.

(ANDREW *wants to interrupt, but* LINDSAY'*s voice is suddenly trembling with emotion.*)

Andrew, we have to. We have to do something. Do we just let the election go down?

(ANDREW *nods, trying to take charge.*)

ANDREW: I see. OK. This is at your initiative?

(LINDSAY *nods.*)

All right. I have to ask you, does Oliver know?

LINDSAY: No.

ANDREW: You want a meeting and you haven't called Oliver?

MARY: Now Andrew . . .

(*But* BRYDEN *looks up sharply before* ANDREW *can go on.*)

BRYDEN: Oliver is absent at my suggestion. If you want to argue, then argue with me.

(*At this* GEORGE *arrives, very fast and silent, in a big coat, followed by* GWENDA *and* TREVOR AVERY. *He goes straight to slump down in a hard chair at the side of the room without acknowledging anyone. He looks exhausted.*)

ANDREW: George . . .

(*There is a silence.* AVERY *moves to take up a nearby position.*)

ANDREW: You look pretty shattered. Are you all right?

GWENDA: George has got ten minutes. I will allow you ten

minutes. Then I insist, he must go to bed.
(GEORGE *smiles weakly*.)

GEORGE: It's true, I must say, I don't feel too wonderful . . .

GWENDA: I'll get you a scotch, George.

MARY: Hold on, there's a bottle out here . . .
(*She runs to get it from a filing cabinet top*, GWENDA *following.*
GEORGE *looks up, grim.*)

GEORGE: Are there new polls?

ANDREW: You don't want to see them. I can't recommend them if
you're not feeling well.
(GEORGE *shakes his head.*)

GEORGE: It doesn't make sense. It makes no sense to me. That's
what I've been thinking, driving all the way back.
Everywhere I go I see people cheering. They're cheering!
(LINDSAY *has sat down quietly, her hands on the big table in
front of her.*)

LINDSAY: But isn't this the problem we have to address?
(GEORGE *looks at her mistrustfully, the freshness of her voice out
of key with his mood.* BRYDEN *looks between them.*)

BRYDEN: Let me be clear, George. This is at my insistence . . .

GEORGE: I see.

BRYDEN: Lindsay came to me. She has a view. She's one step
back from this . . . (*He holds up a hand to prevent* ANDREW
interrupting.) . . . I'm speaking, Andrew . . . so I think she
sees things more clearly.
(*There is a pause.* GWENDA *has the scotch in her hand.*)
And that's why I asked her to put her thoughts straight to
you.
(ANDREW *is shaking his head, unhappy.*)

ANDREW: This is wrong, George. We shouldn't do this. This is
the last thing we need. We have to keep to our structure. It
works. Oliver co-ordinates policy.

BRYDEN: Maybe. But I am Chairman of the Campaign.
(ANDREW *looks nervously at* BRYDEN, *who is in no mood to be
defied.*)

ANDREW: Yes.

BRYDEN: I am an elected representative.

ANDREW: Of course. That's understood. But you know what

we've been trying to do. We've been trying to introduce discipline. Proper organized meetings.

(*He makes square-cut gestures on the table. Suddenly people realize he is cracking from exhaustion.*)

This is not the moment to let that discipline go.

(GEORGE *turns, direct, simple.*)

GEORGE: You mean Lindsay can't even speak?

ANDREW: No, George, I'm not saying that.

GEORGE: Andrew, this isn't Soviet Russia.

(*He says this so quietly that it's scary.* GWENDA *appears beside him.*)

GWENDA: Scotch.

(*He takes the scotch. He turns and gestures at* LINDSAY.)

GEORGE: Lindsay, please go ahead.

(LINDSAY *is ready, absolutely calm.*)

LINDSAY: You see, George, from the beginning, I've had a real problem. The first time I met you, I thought, here's this extraordinary man. In private, articulate, funny, authoritative. Yet who tightens up the minute he goes public, the minute he talks policy.

(ANDREW *has sat down on the edge of the table.* MARY *is watching quietly.* GWENDA *is standing over* GEORGE.)

So the first thing I did was begin to look around you. It's obvious, really. I began to talk to your team. And it's like . . . I don't know . . . it was like they'd forgotten, it was clear they'd lost sight of who you really are.

(ANDREW *looks across to* GEORGE.)

ANDREW: Look . . .

LINDSAY: No, everything they said, it was as if they were trying to protect you. I found I developed that protective mentality myself. (*She smiles at* GEORGE.) I started to see you as a sort of patient in hospital. And like the rest of us I started to behave like I was a nurse.

ANDREW: Now that isn't true.

BRYDEN: I think it is, Andrew.

(ANDREW *turns.* BRYDEN *has sat down at the table, his solid authority unmistakable.*)

LINDSAY: I know it's cowardly to say this when Oliver's not here.

But he does create a certain atmosphere.

RYDEN: He does.

LINDSAY: He creates a nervousness, and I have to say that nervousness has taken its toll.

(GEORGE *is watching, giving nothing away.*)

That night in the studio, I watched you, I realized . . . way before Linus Frank did his trick . . . I thought, this man is trapped. He can only convey one message to the nation: 'Oh God, I hope I don't drop a bollock tonight . . .'

(ANDREW *shakes his head.*)

ANDREW: That's absurd.

LINDSAY: Is it?

ANDREW: You know where this comes from.

LINDSAY: Oh yes, you explained to me. George once made a blunder, what was it, six years ago . . . ?

ANDREW: Not one blunder, Lindsay.

LINDSAY: And for that you still want to punish him. You decided for some reason to smother his wit. All his gaiety. His humour.

(ANDREW *turns away, angry now.*)

ANDREW: Nonsense. That's nonsense.

LINDSAY: And that's why he's angry. Underneath George is always bloody furious. He's angry. And who can blame him?

(GEORGE *watches, giving nothing away.*)

Everything in him wants to let rip.

(ANDREW *looks to* GEORGE, *but* LINDSAY *goes straight on.*)

The public aren't stupid. They know he's been programmed. It's not hard to work out why this man's ratings are low. The public see only one thing when they look at him, and that's six rolls of sticky tape wrapped round his mouth . . .

ANDREW: That's simply not true.

(*She turns, indignant now.*)

LINDSAY: What's wrong with us? Are we really so cynical . . . are we so arrogant, that we truly imagine the public can't tell?

(*But* ANDREW *is holding his ground.*)

ANDREW: I really don't think so. There are good reasons to be careful. The strategy's plain.

LINDSAY: The strategy's ridiculous. Keep George in a box. And meanwhile try to out-Tory the Tories. (*She leans forward, confident.*) But Andrew, finally, I do have to remind you of something you seem to have forgotten. We're not bloody Tories. And so it's a game at which we can't win.
(*She looks at him triumphantly, but* ANDREW *is shaking his head again, every inch the political hard man.*)

ANDREW: We have to do this. We have to. We've worked on this strategy for hour upon hour. Because, like it or not, nobody trusts us to manage the economy. So we must convince them we're good managers now . . . (*He goes on before she can interrupt.*) Yes, and if that does mean a certain greyness, yes, if it means we end up boring . . . OK, I'll live with that. Because this is a policy which has undergone four years' hard graft and four years' refinement . . . (*He looks round, angry.*) Do we throw it out just because one person's wobbling? Christ, there's always wobbling! Do we really throw it out with eight days to go?
(GEORGE *watches, still giving nothing away, as* LINDSAY *shakes her head.*)

LINDSAY: You see it's *this* . . . it's this obsession with our enemy . . . that's been our madness. It leaves us with nothing distinctive. And by this appalling coincidence, it also robs George of what he does best . . . (*She nods.*) George became Leader because of a quality he had. That quality came from his passion.
(GEORGE *is looking hard at her now.*)
Where is that passion tonight?
(*There is a silence. Everyone is watchful.* BRYDEN *is gentle, tactful.*)

BRYDEN: We do have a choice, George. It's whether we think these polls are the start of a trend. If they are, then I think we have to take note of what Lindsay's saying.
(GEORGE *looks at him a moment. Then still holding his scotch he finally speaks.*)

GEORGE: You'd better tell me what you think that means.
(*There is a short silence, everyone holding their breath, the decisive moment reached.*)

92

INDSAY: On Monday night, you're meant to be speaking. It's the first of your three last speeches. Andrew's preparing it now. What he writes . . . you can have in your pocket. So it's there. Like a safety net.

(*There is a silence.* BRYDEN *leans forward slightly.*)

RYDEN: What we want is to hear the George we once knew.

(*Now* BRYDEN *opens his briefcase and takes a volume from it. He puts it down on the table in front of them.* GEORGE *frowns, puzzled.*)

All your major speeches before you were Leader . . .

EORGE: Yes?

RYDEN: When you first started, I often heard you, you wrote nothing down . . .

EORGE: Yes, that right. (*He smiles.*) My father . . . my own father taught me. He said to me: speak, just speak from the heart.

RYDEN: And you did.

EORGE: Without notes, that's right. On the backs of envelopes. Like a Quaker, I simply stood up . . . (*He remembers a moment. Then he lifts a hand and mimes drawing words down from the sky.*) And when I stood up, the words always came. (*He thinks a moment. Then he smiles.*) And then people said to me, now you're the Leader, everything you say must be written down. (*He shrugs and makes a despairing face to say all was then lost.*) From then on . . .

(*The whole group sit quiet now, stilled.*)

RYDEN: George. Why can't you go back?

(*There is a silence between them.*)

Speak. (*He waits.*) Speak. That's your talent. Get up on Monday and say what you want. Say it without thinking. Just say it. (*He looks straight at* GEORGE.) The Bible and Shakespeare. That's where you started . . .

EORGE: Yes.

RYDEN: I remember. I heard you speak many times. These were your texts. Not the public sector borrowing requirement. All that bollocks, whatever it is. People don't know. But they do know injustice. And they see it in their own lives . . . (*He shakes his head.*) When people ask the modern Labour Party

the time, we seem to answer, I don't know, what time would you
like it to be?
(*Now* GEORGE *smiles too.*)
But there's a whole group of people. They've been
abandoned. Nobody speaks for them. No one speaks in their
language. Because no one's willing to talk about hope . . .
(*He leans in across the table.*) It's like we're embarrassed.
Why? What's the reason?
(GEORGE *is staring at him now.*)
People are waiting to hear from you. That's the feeling out
there. They want to see you go for it. They want to see you
take the whole rotten thing on.
(GEORGE *thinks a moment, then he gets up and moves across the*
room, his scotch in his hand, thinking. BRYDEN *sits back.*)
That's what they want. Not bloody economics class. Which
we all know you don't understand.
GEORGE: Well thank you, Bryden.
(*There is a pause.* GWENDA *is hovering tactfully behind him.*
Then he moves across to ANDREW *and holds out his hand for the*
speech ANDREW *has prepared. He takes it, and then smiles.*)
You come, you arrive like temptation, with the impossible
message. You come and tell me: just be yourself, George.
(*He looks at them a moment. They all smile as he puts his hat on*
and hurries back into the night, GWENDA *and* TREVOR
following.)

SCENE EIGHT

The Manchester Rally. Night. The sound of the Labour theme tune
swelling over huge speakers to cut into the excited crowd. There is a big
stage with the words IT'S YOUR LABOUR PARTY. *Glaring spotlights*
find GEORGE *who is standing at a lectern, in the middle of his speech,*
addressing an audience of thousands in an arena. Above him hangs an
enormous screen which projects him live to the crowd, as at a rock
concert, so that the small figure at the lectern is overwhelmed by his
own image. The cheering dies as he reaches out across the arena,
coming in high and loud, speaking without notes. The effect of the

loudspeakers is to make every word separate, punched out, huge in the night.

GEORGE: I am asked a lot – a lot of people ask me – what are your roots? What is your root reason for being a socialist? And what does socialism mean to you now?

We have in this country, I say, one party whose whole interest is in giving still more to those who already have. To those that have shall more be given. I can never get past the intellectual disgrace of that idea!

(*There is a considerable rumble of approval at this from the large crowd.* GEORGE *looks up, searching for the next phrase.*)

It is said to me: there is no longer hope in our future. No sense of potential. No sense of possibility. In our own lifetime, a whole generation has been effectively abandoned and dispossessed. They have been told to fend for themselves.

(*He pauses a moment, then thunders.*)

Comrades, my socialism is the socialism that says these people must not be let go.

(*There is applause. You can see him use the moment to regroup.*)

My socialism is . . . it is concrete. It is real. It is to do with helping people. It is the way in which we go forward now to make this a country in which everyone is helped.

(*There is the disparate applause of an audience which has only half-understood what the speaker has just said and* GEORGE *thunders in on top of it.*)

That is what my socialism is.

It is.

(*There is a slight pause as he embarks, sweating, on a new section. The crowd sounds a little listless.*)

It is an enabling philosophy. It is something by which something gets done. It is the means of doing something. That is what it is. And that is what it will be.

(*The words are beginning to slide and there is only scattered applause at this. He hits each of the following words.*)

Having said that, so let me please now. To give you the idea. Let me . . . say, it is there, it is in me, it is the core, and at the

95

core you will find this belief: this belief: that I will not let one of you down.
I will not.
(*He shakes his head slightly, then he stops and looks up towards the sky. A silence which seems to go on for ever.*)
So . . .
Now . . .
Let me . . .
Now . . .
Let me continue. I have here the words.
(*He reaches, sweating profusely now and rather clumsily for some folded up pieces of paper from inside his jacket. He has a moment's panic as his hands shake unfolding them.*)
In my pocket. I have them.
(*There is a silence. Then he steadies himself before he thunders out again, with absolute authority once more, from the safety of the notes.*)
Let me read you the words I came here to say.

SCENE NINE

The Manchester rally. Backstage. GEORGE *comes off the stage, gladhanding his way through the crowd, smiling and laughing in the very distance as* ANDREW *comes on at the front ready to meet him and plainly concerned. There are two enormous doors at the very back through which* GEORGE *now quickly comes, heading for the big darkened backstage area, followed by* TREVOR.

GEORGE: Just get me a drink . . .
ANDREW: All right . . .
GEORGE: Please get me a drink out here . . .
    (*He is taking his jacket off and shaking his head, mad, wild and soaked through.*)
ANDREW: It's all right, George, it was absolutely fine. It was fine.
    (*He has moved across quickly to stand opposite him and is meanwhile throwing a nervous look towards the door through*

96

which MARY *is coming quickly. Behind her you can see people milling about outside the doors.*)

GEORGE: It showed.

ANDREW: Yes it showed just for a moment. We weren't live. We weren't live on television. Just for a moment we lost you out there.

(MARY *is standing on the other side of him now, trying equally to reassure him.*)

MARY: It's all right, George, I promise you.

GEORGE: I do need a drink. I also need a cigarette.

ANDREW: Yes. Get him both.

(MARY *heads off at once to get scotch and cigarettes.* TREVOR *goes out to case the waiting crowd.* GEORGE *shakes his head.*)

GEORGE: I just can't do it.

ANDREW: George, you can do it.

GEORGE: No, it's gone. The bloody thing's gone.

(GWENDA *has come through the doors and is standing a few feet away.*)

GWENDA: There's a crowd out here, there's the Mayor of Manchester . . .

ANDREW: Later, Gwenda, he'll see them later.

(*But he has moved away, opening his shirt which is drenched.*)

GEORGE: There's nothing you can say. You can't say anything. You're not allowed to say anything. How can I say what I feel in my heart?

(MARY *has returned.* GWENDA *has gone to deal with the waiting crowd outside the doors.*)

MARY: The drink is here.

GEORGE: All those hours in hotel rooms working at speeches, drafting, re-drafting, polishing, changing every word and all you're doing is covering up for what's really gone wrong. What you know in your heart. What really happened. What *really* happened . . .

(*He pauses a moment. The others are suddenly still in the middle of his stream of consciousness.*)

You once had the words. Now you don't.

(*He stands, naked to the waist, the glass in his hand.* MARY *holds out the clean shirt as* ANDREW *looks across alarmed to her.*)

97

GWENDA: George, I'm sorry, there's a whole crew out there. Also delegations from the local Labour Parties . . .

MARY: George . . .

(*But* GEORGE *has walked away again, not even getting into the shirt.*)

GEORGE: I got up there, I thought all the things I truly care about . . . Northern Ireland. What can you say? You can't say anything. Not publicly. The whole bloody country's been bleeding for years . . .

MARY: I know . . .

(GWENDA *is calling to the people waiting outside the doors.*)

GWENDA: He's coming. He really is coming.

GEORGE: It's been dying and we can't speak, we can't say anything, you're not allowed to say *anything*.

ANDREW: No, I know, it's a problem.

(*They wait tactfully beside him.* GWENDA *has returned.*)

GWENDA: George, the Mayor is outside.

(GEORGE *shakes his head again.*)

GEORGE: I thought, you know, out there I was thinking, Northern Ireland, it's 'above politics'. That's what we say. Well what sort of politics is it which says that certain things are too important to be spoken of?

(GWENDA *calls to the people outside as* MARY *slips the shirt on to him, putting his cigarette in her own mouth as she does so. But he turns, his contempt frightening.*)

GEORGE: So what are we left with? All the other stuff is a game.

GWENDA: He is coming, I promise you . . .

(*He shakes his head, gentler now, following his thoughts.*)

GEORGE: We can't speak of history, you can't say Britain happens to be trapped in historical decline. You can't even say that. But it's true. You'd only have to say it and the whole bloody roof would blow off!

MARY: George . . .

(*He absently takes the cigarette from her and wanders away, she following to do up his cuffs.*)

GEORGE: Defence! Abandoning nuclear weapons, which everyone knows we should do, I could make a great speech about that. My God! If only I could! But of course if I say it, that's fifty thousand jobs . . .

ANDREW: Of course . . .

GEORGE: It's real people's livelihoods . . .

(GWENDA *has appeared again beside him.*)

GWENDA: George, I wonder, could I have a word?

(*But he is suddenly off again, the passion rising in him once more.*)

GEORGE: Not to mention the economy, I can't talk of the economy, we've found that already, say anything truthful, the whole gaff is blown . . . (*He turns.*) I can't say anything. I can't say I don't like Germans. I can't say I'm not feeling well. I'm angry, I'm impatient. I can't even say the Welsh drive me mad.

GWENDA: Thanks, George.

(*But he does not even notice, inflamed again now.* TREVOR *has come back through the main door.*)

GEORGE: Not to mention the royal bloody family . . . hereditary peerages, my God, what shred of intellectual justification can there be . . .

TREVOR: Is he coming?

GWENDA: He is.

GEORGE: We live in a country which is spavined with ancestor-worship. This country will never, *can* never prosper until it escapes from its past. (*He turns and addresses them all.*) Why can't I say that? You tell me. What is this? Is this my fault? Or is it the public's? (*He turns back away from them.*) Why can't I speak of what I believe?

(*But suddenly* GWENDA *speaks, raging with unsuspected anger from the other side of the room.*)

GWENDA: There is a list, I do have to tell you, George, there is a list, there is a queue of people out there. Listen to me, George, they number a hundred. They all need to see you, they all need to talk to you.

(*The worm has turned and the whole room stands astonished.*)
You have to tell them it's all going well . . .

(*She has suddenly shouted this last instruction at him. And he looks back at her with a mad intensity in his eye.*)

GEORGE: Well it is! It's all going wonderfully! Everything's going absolutely great! Within the confines of what I may say to them, I am bloody well doing as well as I can!

(*They all look round. He suddenly seems slightly mad.*)

ANDREW: Yes. You are. You are making an impact.

MARY: He's doing very well.

ANDREW: Yes he is.

GEORGE: Except I'm not allowed to say anything. Apart from that I'm doing fine.

(*He pulls on his jacket. He stands, restored.*)

MARY: OK?

GEORGE: All right, good, right, good, right then everyone, we get back to it. Right, here we go. We open the doors. We continue.

(*He pauses.* GWENDA *goes to the door.* MARY *points nervously to the smoking cigarette in his hand.*)

MARY: I'm sorry. No fag, George.

(*He looks at her a moment. Then hands it to her.*)

GEORGE: Open the door and get back to work.

(*She opens the door. Outside there is an almighty babble of people and lights. It freezes for a moment as it sees him, and then as he and* TREVOR *advance towards the doors, it moves forward to engulf him. As the doors close, the light on stage begins to die.*)

ANDREW: Keep out there, be sure, just keep with him . . .

MARY: I will . . .

ANDREW: Just keep by his side . . .

MARY: He's OK, he's doing fine.

ANDREW: Yes. Absolutely.

(GWENDA *and* MARY *have gone.* ANDREW *stands a moment, alone in the darkened and stilled arena.*

Then from the other side LINDSAY *appears and stands opposite him, looking across the huge area towards him. He looks at her and does not need to say anything. Instead he just stands, bitter, hostile.*)

Thank you, Lindsay. Put him back in the box.

(*The stage darkens as he heads towards the doors.*)

SCENE TEN

Outside a Birmingham hotel ballroom. MARY *steps forward to address us directly. She is carrying a cup of coffee.*

MARY: Everyone always asks how he was on polling day. 'You were with him. How did he feel? Did he know? Had he guessed which way the election would go?'
The fact is, he was free. That was the irony. Just for that afternoon, as he walked across the parks in his own constituency, he found the freedom he'd always sought. He knew by evening he'd be back on the roller-coaster. Events would pick him up and throw him down. But just for a few hours, it was truly peaceful. For those few hours, history leaves you alone.

SCENE ELEVEN

The lights have come up behind MARY *and revealed a ballroom in a Birmingham hotel which has been commandeered by the Labour Party. The room is huge, ornate, gilded, mirrored. Now it is empty but for a selection of gilt chairs.* GEORGE *is sitting alone, dreaming, smoking a cigarette.* GWENDA *is sitting against the back wall, a long way from him, just waiting.* TREVOR *is some way away.* MARY *walks across the ballroom and hands* GEORGE *the cup of coffee which he takes with an absent smile.* MARY *moves quietly across the room and goes out of the big gilded doors.*
There is a long silence, GEORGE *sitting smoking,* GWENDA *a great distance away from him and also not moving. Time goes by.*
Then, after a while OLIVER *slips in the big door. He closes it and moves a few paces into the room to stand near* GEORGE. GEORGE *looks up at him.*

GEORGE: It's no, isn't it?
    (OLIVER *just nods very slightly.* GEORGE *looks away.*)
    It isn't there. That's what I suspected.
    (OLIVER *opens his hands slightly, as if to apologize for not*

having better news.)

I suspected the other thing too. I suspected both things. Winning and losing. Equally. (*He looks up at* OLIVER.) By how many?

OLIVER: Twenty or thirty, I think.

(GEORGE *nods.*)

I mean, you know . . . it's only the exit polls. It's not unknown for them to be wrong . . .

(GEORGE *holds his hand up, not wanting consolation.*)

But it's true, it's not a good omen.

(*There is a pause.* OLIVER *throws a quick glance over at* GWENDA *who is sitting stunned at the back, not moving. He looks at his watch.*)

Five minutes past ten. Do you want me to stay with you?

GEORGE: Yes. Just for a while.

(OLIVER *goes and sits in his coat on another of the gilt ballroom chairs. There is a silence. Then* GWENDA *gets up and walks out of the room, saying nothing.* OLIVER *shakes his head.*)

OLIVER: Do you know what I hate? I hate what they'll do to you. They'll all start to say you were a great man. 'Oh what a great man!' they'll say. Now they've disposed of you. (*He shakes his head slightly.*) Now the threat's over, they'll crown you with praise . . .

(GEORGE, *dragging on his cigarette, looks across at him.*)

GEORGE: I'm sorry, Oliver. I've felt very badly. About what happened between us, I mean . . .

OLIVER: Forget it.

GEORGE: I don't think we'll know . . . I mean, I can't tell what would have happened if we'd stuck together. If we'd done things differently.

(OLIVER *looks at him, his voice toughening slightly.*)

OLIVER: What would have happened? I'll tell you . . .

(*There is a pause.* OLIVER *smiles slightly, the poignancy of the moment given a sudden twist.*)

We would have won.

(GEORGE *looks away,* OLIVER's *brutal straightness too much for him now.*)

GEORGE: Well . . .

(*But* OLIVER *goes on, not relenting.*)

OLIVER: Oh yes I know, I'm sure you think it's more complicated. I'm sure you think it's not as simple as that. But we both know. We both have a secret, George. We could have won this. It was there for the winning. And I'll never forgive us if we've thrown it away . . .

(GEORGE *looks at him about to speak but* OLIVER *interrupts at once.*)

GEORGE: Look . . .

OLIVER: You know what it was. You should have seen Malcolm.

GEORGE: I did. I saw Malcolm.

OLIVER: You should have seen Malcolm six months ago. And if he wouldn't back you, if he wouldn't come out for you hot, strong and cheering, you should have sacked him. You should have fixed him.

GEORGE: Should I?

OLIVER: Of course. I've heard you so often. In a fifty-fifty you always say you could do it. You can pull the trigger, that's what you say. But you can't. Let's face it. When it actually comes to it, you don't have the nerve.

(GEORGE *looks at him a moment, toughening now, not at all defensive.*)

GEORGE: I could have moved, yes, I could have moved against him. I could have made him put up or get out. But if I had, I'd have handed him a weapon. And he would have played it for all it was worth.

OLIVER: You should have done it.

(GEORGE *looks at him, his own voice steelier, stronger.*)

GEORGE: I know. You say that. It's easy for you. But I have to think of something else. I have to think of the Party.

OLIVER: The Party? My God!

GEORGE: Yes. (*He pauses a moment, as if finding comfort in what he will say.*) I believe in it.

OLIVER: And where have we landed the Party tonight?

(OLIVER *turns away in disgust. But* GEORGE *just shakes his head sadly.*)

GEORGE: That isn't the point. That isn't it finally. Malcolm is the next Leader this party will have. I had to hand him the Party in good order.

(OLIVER *is looking at him in disbelief.*)

OLIVER: Good order? *Good order?* (*He is beginning to raise his voice.*) And that's why you let him get away with so much? (GEORGE *looks at him a moment.*)
You endured his sneering, his laughing with all his Oxford bloody colleagues . . .

GEORGE: Yes.

OLIVER: You put up with him schmoozing with journalists, leaking, spreading leaks behind your back . . .

GEORGE: Yes.

OLIVER: Rolling his eyes when you spoke in Shadow Cabinet, going out and subverting younger MPs . . .
(GEORGE *looks at him unapologetic.*)

GEORGE: Yes.

OLIVER: You put up with all that so you can hand him the Party in *reasonable condition*?

GEORGE: Yes. Yes. (*He looks up at* OLIVER *not flinching.*) As it happens, I did.
(OLIVER *gets up, indignant now, his disbelief turning to anger.*)

OLIVER: And now . . . what? . . . *now* this man will inherit. You sit there and face that without wanting to get up and seize him by the throat?

GEORGE: Yes I do.

OLIVER: Oh I can see it. You are going to support him. I know you, George. You'll offer him support!

GEORGE: Of course I will.
(OLIVER *moves away, enraged.*)

OLIVER: You call this strength? It's the most miserable weakness. (*He turns from across the ballroom.*) You will give him a loyalty he never gave you.
(GEORGE *is calm, not yielding to* OLIVER *an inch.*)

GEORGE: I have to. Yes. Because I believe in the Party. I'm not sentimental. The Party is not my whole life. But it's all we have. It's the only practical instrument that exists in this country for changing people's lives for the good. Yes. And if I'd followed my quarrel, if I'd pursued my enemy right to the end, split the party in two, had screaming headlines – LABOUR'S LEADING FIGURES FALL OUT – my God, what vanity! What self-indulgence! The very self-indulgence I condemn in everyone else . . . (*He is still.*) So I've eaten crow. That's been my diet. I've bitten back the tongue in my mouth. I've done it consciously. Knowing just what I was doing. And knowing what the price was as well. (*His gaze is steady.*) It's been my decision. I'll live with it. (*He turns and suddenly looks hard at* OLIVER.) And I'll live with what you think of me too.

(OLIVER *nods, suddenly quiet.*)

OLIVER: Well, I'll tell you one thing. I know what will happen. In six or eight hours you will appear, you will make your emotional appearance at five in the morning. You will stand on the steps outside Walworth Road. And that well-known eloquence which has so far eluded you, I know, I tell you, you wait, I can just hear it, as if by magic it will all come flooding back . . .

(GEORGE *looks round resentfully at him as* OLIVER *begins to move towards him.*)

Oh yes, I can see it! This is the occasion! This is the one you're going to get right! Your finest hour! Oh never happier than fighting Dunkirk! (*He is suddenly intense, quiet.*) Well, you must know . . . please think . . . as you're standing there . . . as you stand on those steps, as you look at all those party workers who love you, with the tears in their eyes, weeping once more for how moving you are . . . please remember there'll be one man out there who isn't bloody crying. (*He suddenly raises his voice.*) Because you'll be doing the one thing Labour Leaders are best at. Oh yes, George. You'll be conceding defeat. (*He spits out the words in contempt, as angry at himself as at* GEORGE.) I won't bloody cry. Why should I? One more Labour Leader who was insufficiently ruthless . . . Another leaky vessel for the hopes of the Left . . . (*He turns, bitter.*) I always admired your love of the military. I thought you admired them because they got the job done. But it wasn't love, George. It wasn't love, was it?

(*He smiles.*) It was jealousy. They have something you don't. It was you, George, after all you were the first Labour Leader . . . it was you who always said: a new philosophy!

Power at all costs! Power before everything! Power's the only thing that counts! *And you didn't get it . . .* (*He is suddenly quiet.*) So what does that leave you with?

(GEORGE *looks up at him, mild.*)

GEORGE: It leaves me with not very much.

(*At once* MARY *appears at the door. She is nervous, on the point of tears.*)

MARY: George . . .

GEORGE: You all right?

(*She nods.*)

MARY: Yes. I'm sorry to bother you. It's just . . . I'm sorry . . . we need a new line.

(GEORGE *nods, grave.*)

GEORGE: Ah yes, of course . . .

MARY: I mean, I know that it's early, we still don't have any actual results. But we do need a statement. I've drawn up something . . .

GEORGE: Ah yes . . .

(*She moves forward. There are now tears in her eyes.*)

MARY: This is something for you to approve.

(*He takes it from her, blind to it, not really knowing what it is.*)

GEORGE: Yes, I see.

MARY: The gist is, you see, they have no moral mandate. Even if they do win the seats. That's what we're saying . . .

GEORGE: Yes.

MARY: No one's a winner.

GEORGE: Quite.

MARY: Because over half the people didn't vote for them . . . (*She pauses, choking now.*) So the point is, they have no moral right . . .

(OLIVER *just watches, pitiless at the side of the room, as* MARY *and* GEORGE *become equally choked.*)

GEORGE: No.

MARY: We do need to put this out on the bleeper. I've got to lay down a line . . . (*She is having trouble speaking.*) It's essential. It's absolutely essential . . .

(*She has begun to cry, the tension of the weeks overwhelming her, tears pouring down her face.*)

GEORGE: Now Mary . . .

MARY: It's vital . . . it's vital . . . all Labour candidates must say the same thing.

(GEORGE *stands to reach out to her, but she steps back, shaking her head. The door opens.* GWENDA *is standing outside with* ANDREW. OLIVER *takes one look, then he turns and walks out of the room.*)

GWENDA: George . . .

GEORGE: Yes?

GWENDA: We've made the arrangements.

(MARY *turns and goes quickly out with her document.*)

ANDREW: We think you'll concede about four o'clock.

GWENDA: The car's standing by . . .

GEORGE: Good.

GWENDA: To take you to London as soon as you have your own result.

(*He nods.* LINDSAY *has now also appeared in the doorway. She is in tears.*)

LINDSAY: Excuse me, George.

GEORGE: Yes?

LINDSAY: I was thinking . . . perhaps . . . as we have to wait . . . would you like me to help? Should we start working on what you will say?

(*They all stand, stunned a moment, as a* WAITRESS *comes in. She looks round, then points at* GEORGE's *feet. She has a Birmingham accent.*)

WAITRESS: Is this yours?

GEORGE: I'm sorry?

WAITRESS: Are you going to pick that cup off the floor?

(*He realizes what she is saying and bends down to pick up the coffee cup.*)

You're not anyone special. Just because you're who you are.

GEORGE: No. No, I know.

WAITRESS: You can still say thank you.

GEORGE: Yes.

(*The others stand watching in a group, unable to move.*)

Yes. Thank you.

WAITRESS: It makes no difference to me.

(*She turns and goes out, pleased with the impact she's made. At the door now* MARY *has returned and is standing alongside* GWENDA, LINDSAY, ANDREW *and* TREVOR.)

ANDREW: Perhaps we should go.

GEORGE: Yes. (*He nods.*) Yes, well I'm ready.

ANDREW: Your own vote's higher than ever before.

GEORGE: I see.

ANDREW: I mean, they're saying in your own constituency your majority's larger than ever, they say.

(GEORGE *moves towards the door. But before he gets there he stops. A sudden access of energy.*)

GEORGE: You know what I think? I think, let's all just be Tories. After all, they always win. So what's the point of having other parties? Given that they never get in?

(*There are some nervous smiles from the group, not knowing quite how seriously to take him.*)

Whereas, you know, if we join the Tory Party, we could do something. I'm beginning to think it's our best chance. Why not? (*He smiles and suddenly turns, reaching out his arms to them.*) Let's join the Tory Party. And then let's all fuck it up.

(*He laughs. The others laugh. Then he reaches out his arms and puts them round their shoulders as they turn and go out the door.*)

SCENE TWELVE

Outside Downing Street. It is 5 a.m. and still pitch dark. Once more the microphone has been set up. On either side of it are two small Christmas trees with fairy lights. It is beginning to snow. A circle of cameramen, journalists and supporters is standing round as CHARLES KENDRICK *walks across the road accompanied by his wife* CAROLE. *They are blue with cold.*

KENDRICK: I would like to say how happy this moment makes me. It has been hard pounding. The nightmare of a Labour government has now receded and Britain, thank goodness, this distraction over, can settle down and get back to work. I would like to add a word about my opponent, for whom this result is a personal tragedy, of course. We have had our differences. But I know I and my wife Carole both feel in essence he is a decent and honourable man.

I have to say news has only today reached me, informing of just how grave the economic situation is – perhaps graver than we have recently thought. That means we shall be busy even in what we now know may be difficult times ahead.

Meanwhile, thank you for your confidence. Merry Christmas. Goodnight.

SCENE THIRTEEN

At once the massed bands begin to play Nimrod from Elgar's Variations. The Cenotaph. Onto the stage come the soldiers, the sailors, the airmen, the diplomats, re-creating the image of the first scene.

The music plays. The three political leaders enter, wreaths in hand. They are now CHARLES KENDRICK, MALCOLM PRYCE *and the* LIBERAL LEADER. *They stand, waiting in silence. The music stops. There is complete still. Then, through the crowd comes* GEORGE, *not dressed for the occasion but in his usual clothes. He addresses us in the silence.*

GEORGE: My own mother died. She died in an air-raid. In South London, during the blitz. It's almost my very first memory, my aunts weeping as they gave me the news.

And since then . . . fifty years' honest endeavour. Fifty years doing my best. Being told everything I love and value no longer meets the needs of the day.

(*There is silence. The crowd stirs.*)

In the year since my own bruising experience I have found myself asking a question which will always haunt us and to which no easy answer appears.

(*He pauses.*)

Is this history? Is everything history? Could we have done more? Was it possible? And how shall we know?
(*The massed bands of the army play Purcell's* WHEN I AM LAID TO EARTH, MAY MY SINS CREATE NO TROUBLE IN MY BREAST . . .
The company remain frozen as the lights fade and the music swells.)